PROCLAMATION

L E N T

**INTERPRETING
THE LESSONS OF
THE CHURCH YEAR**

CAIN HOPE FELDER

**PROCLAMATION 5
SERIES A**

FORTRESS PRESS   MINNEAPOLIS

This book is dedicated to
my sister Patience Olivia Brown
and
my brother Robbie Jackson Felder

PROCLAMATION 5
Interpreting the Lessons of the Church Year
Series A, Lent

Cover and interior design: Spangler Design Team

Library of Congress Cataloging-in-Publication Data

Proclamation 5 : interpreting the lessons of the church year.
    p. cm.
    Contents: ser. A. [1] Epiphany / Pheme Perkins. [2] Holy week /
Robert H. Smith. [3] Advent/Christmas / Mark Allan Powell.
[4] Lent / Cain Hope Felder.
    ISBN 0-8006-4178-7 (ser. A, Epiphany) — ISBN
0-8006-4180-9 (ser. A, Holy week) — ISBN 0-8006-4177-9
(ser. A, Advent/Christmas) — ISBN 0-8006-4179-5 (ser. A, Lent)
    1. Bible—Homiletical use. 2. Bible—Liturgical lessons, English.
BS534.5.P765 1992
251—dc20   92-22973
                                                                          CIP

The paper used in this publication meets the minimum requirements of American National Standard for Information Services—Permanence of Paper for Printed Library Materials, ANSI Z329.48-1984. ∞™

Manufactured in the U.S.A.   AF 1-4179
96   95   94   93   92   1   2   3   4   5   6   7   8   9   10

CONTENTS

Preface

The tradition of making special preparations for "holy convocation" is very ancient indeed. The religious calendar events of the early Hebrews and Jews are frequently noticed in the Old Testament, while those of Islam are evident even within the Qur'an. From its earliest existence the Christian church began to develop its own distinctive calendar of holy convocations or seasons, and Lent is one of the most significant, as this book attempts to demonstrate. Not surprisingly, the Bible is foundational for systematic reflection during the Lenten season. When ancient texts intersect with the modern context in a purposeful way, new life can be breathed into the erstwhile routine of daily religious practice.

This book is the result of sustained reflection, not just on my part as author, but on the part of others of different denominations who have assisted me with their ideas. I am grateful for their assistance and collaboration without which it would have been most difficult to finish in a timely fashion. Thus, I wish to thank formally J. Michael West, Marshall Johnson, David Lott, Charles Puskas, and Timothy Staveteig for their assistance. A special word of thanks is also in order to my secretary, Joy Marie Dufour, and to my colleagues and students at Howard University School of Divinity for putting up with my absences as I worked on this volume.

CAIN HOPE FELDER

Introduction

Increasing number of pastors and other Christian leaders are recognizing today a critical need for spiritual disciplines. These include prayer, meditation, fasting, miniretreats, and even creative ways for celebrating the power of the Holy Spirit. In this regard, the season of Lent is becoming more and more prominent on the program calendars of a growing number of church communions. Lent has become important again—perhaps especially so because the present age confronts the individual and groups with so many socio-economic and political pressures and everyday stresses that demand relief, if we are to cope and function coherently in modern society.

This book is meant to be a biblical resource for preachers and worship leaders, but I do not simply impose a single "red thread" or some governing image (other than what God's grace has done for us all through the sacrifices of Christ Jesus) for this set of Lenten biblical texts. Instead, I invite the preacher to think with me regarding the different themes that I have discerned from Ash Wednesday, from each Sunday in Lent, and from the overall worship context. Part of this "thinking together" means that the reader is encouraged to familiarize himself or herself with the full content of this book as a solid way to prepare for the Lenten season. In this way, readers will maximize the usefulness of this book and identify best those ways it may serve as a resource for worship and spiritual disciplines appropriate for this season.

THEMES

Ash Wednesday

The notions of penance and sacrifice traditionally associated with Ash Wednesday are not popular today, especially since they often convey the idea of punishment. Nevertheless, these ancient disciplines constitute the prerequisites for receiving a fresh start. In each lesson, the message is similar: Return now to God and adopt a life worthy of God.

First Sunday in Lent

The Lenten sojourn of spiritual discipline is announced as *imitatio Christi*—imitating Christ. These biblical texts usher listeners into a minidrama on the gift of paradise, on the tragedy of "paradise lost," and on the gift of paradise regained by taking seriously God's grace in the Christ-event. The genuine basis for a renewed covenant is buttressed by Jesus' own example and its implications: Go and do likewise.

Second Sunday in Lent

When God's calls come, persons are often caught between the comfortably familiar and the terrifyingly new. Some respond without hesitation; others seem overwhelmed. For those who seize or are seized by God's call, the resulting faith is personal and at odds with the seeming reality.

Third Sunday in Lent

This Sunday focuses on the faithfulness of God to all who are in need. Yet this emphasis is decidedly not individualistic; these texts also speak of God's relationship to those in right relations with others, that is, in community. In each lesson humankind is claimed as God's own.

Fourth Sunday in Lent

The texts ask the question, Are not all the judgments of God in human affairs ultimately occasions for rejoicing? The ways of God confront and challenge human standards and expectations. The cause for celebration—for rejoicing—is this reversal of the usual, human view of this world.

Fifth Sunday in Lent

The biblical passages point not to individual resurrection but to the lost hope and separation, even bondage, that many persons experience in the present. This needs to be addressed with a word of hope and liberation, with both spiritual and social implications for all.

WORSHIP CONTEXT

The term *lent* has its origin in the Anglo-Saxon word *lencten*, which referred to the "lengthening" of the daylight hours, that is, spring. This term was connected to the Christian focus on the self-sacrifice and redemptive sufferings of Jesus in the season of fasting, penance, and self-sacrifice prior to Easter Sunday. The season has been associated with the period of instruction for catechumenates prior to baptism on Easter and with a prescribed fast as a part of that instruction. That Moses, Elijah, and Jesus underwent fasts of forty days also seems significant for the development of this season and its association with acts of sacrifice.

In the West, Irenaeus seems to be the first to mention a period of three weeks; in the East, this observance was extended to six or even seven weeks. Canon 5 of the Council of Nicea (325 c.e.) is the first church text to mention the period of forty days. Nicea also established the range of dates in which Easter could fall—any Sunday between March 22 and April 25. It could not occur on the fourteenth of Nisan, on Passover, or on March 21, the spring equinox.

Gregory the Great, in 604 c.e., inaugurated Ash Wednesday (*Dies Cinerum*, "the day of ashes"), when Christians were expected to sprinkle ashes and repent. Ashes are a long-established biblical symbol for mourning, penitence, humiliation, and purification. This reinforced Lent as a season for self-examination, self-testing, and self-sacrifice.

For centuries, Catholic and Eastern Orthodox churches established regular ritual observances for the Lenten season. Many of the Reformation traditions maintained such observance, and more recently Protestant denominations such as the African Methodist Episcopal, A.M.E. Zion, and National Progressive Baptists (all three being black denominations) have adopted elements of such practices, increasingly making regular use of the lectionary approach to Christian observances.

Even though such increasing signs of unity are commendable within Christendom, pastors are responsible to allow the gospel free reign in adapting to communal circumstances and needs. Toward this challenge for thoughtful innovation and creativity, I offer these interpretations as a companion to each Christian community's life and worship.

Ash Wednesday

Lutheran	Roman Catholic	Episcopal	Common Lectionary
Joel 2:12-19	Joel 2:12-18	Joel 2:1-2, 12-17	Joel 2:1-2, 12-17a
2 Cor. 5:20b—6:2	2 Cor. 5:20—6:2	2 Cor. 5:20b—6:10	2 Cor. 5:20b—6:2 (3-10)
Matt. 6:1-6, 16-21	Matt. 6:1-6, 16-18	Matt. 6:1-6, 16-21	Matt. 6:1-6, 16-21

Penance (originally *poena*, "punishment") and sacrifice are not popular or welcomed notions in contemporary church life. Often, today, punishment is understood as what the individual is presently experiencing and needs to resolve: One needs to drop "codependencies," heal the "inner child," and so forth. Although such coming to terms with one's past is important, and although current therapies and self-help programs have proved beneficial, one should not confuse these with Ash Wednesday, especially if this day is in any way associated with punishment. Similarly, religious confession can become so truncated, routinized, even impersonal, that its repetition does not lead to contrition or a desire to change.

Yet, penance and sacrifice constitute the prerequisites for receiving a fresh start, as the biblical texts for this day make clear. The prophet Joel, aware of present or impending calamities, calls the people to don sackcloth and ashes and asserts the hope that "everyone who calls on the name of the Lord shall be saved" (2:32a). Paul admonishes his readers in Corinth to be reconciled to (literally, "to become friends with") God and one another. Matthew warns against public spectacles of one's piety, good works, prayers, fasting, or treasures because one either stores up praise and treasures in public—its own reward—or one stores up secret treasures about which only God knows. In each lesson, the message is similar: Return now to God and adopt a life worthy of God. This is the message of Ash Wednesday.

FIRST LESSON: JOEL 2:1-2, 12-19

Joel, the Old Testament prophet, is a shadowy figure historically. We know that he lived in Judah around the fifth century (ca. 450—

350 B.C.E.). The book that bears his name (literally, "God is" or "the Lord is God") is a postexilic text; that is, it was written after the Temple in Jerusalem had been rebuilt. Joel alerts his readers to an impending disaster already unfolding in the massive "plague of locusts" (1:4-10), which probably is more than a metaphor. The image of locusts is reminiscent of the eighth plague upon the Egyptian pharaoh (Exod. 10:1-20), in which these insects represented an instrument of God's judgment against the hard-hearted pharaoh. (Unlike various grasshoppers, locusts have the capacity to swarm and mass migrate long distances.) In contrast to the Exodus-event, Joel pictures the locusts as personifying a "powerful nation" (Joel 1:6) that is igniting a great conflagration upon Judah (1:19-20; 2:3, 5).

Even though it seems to be the eleventh hour, Joel issues a call to repentance (1:13-14). What are the sins or offenses committed by the people? Joel does not say. For what reason is God's terrible wrath ignited? We do not learn the answer. This conflagration by another nation is connected to the day of the Lord (2:1-2, 11b), meaning the time of God's apocalyptic judgment and harsh punishment of Judah's inhabitants. This is cause to sound the trumpets and assemble the inhabitants.

Whatever the causes of offense—and prophetic literature in both the Hebrew Bible and the New Testament is often sketchy in this regard—the writer is clearly upset, and the community is obviously in trouble. Here, Joel assumes that his original hearers will know precisely the reasons for such a severe rebuke and even destruction.

Joel 2:12-19 marks an abrupt shift from apocalyptic doom and woe to what might be called apocalyptic hope for those willing to listen, confess, repent, and change. Notice the twofold imperatives (vv. 12-13): "Return to me with all your heart" (*lev* in Hebrew includes mind and heart [see Ps. 51:10]) and "return to the Lord, your God." These invitations presuppose that the Temple stands; God has allowed it to be rebuilt. Evidently, the standing Temple itself is not enough; more concrete actions are expected from believers. Perhaps the people have scarcely done enough to demonstrate the genuineness of their belief in God's grace, mercy, and steadfast love. The commands to "sanctify a fast," to "call a solemn assembly," and to "sanctify the congregation" (vv. 15-16) suggest that erstwhile fasts and religious gatherings have been superficial, if not hypocritical. Even now, Joel insists that it is not too late to start over.

Strikingly, Joel refers to the inner court of the priests (v. 17; literally, "between the vestibule and the altar"). This is the location where a demoralized or complaisant clergy needs to be urged to contrition on behalf of the people. The priests' only concern seems to be that others will ridicule their desolation (i.e., "the plague of locusts") as a sign of the ineffectiveness of their God. The priestly vision has itself been blurred, but the prophet Joel seeks to assist the priests in regaining clear sight. In Joel 2:18-19, the prophet reiterates the promise of hope from God. Plagues, even this devastation, can be overcome; the divine interest is for the people of God to enjoy "grain, wine, and oil," ancient indications of domestic prosperity.

This apocalyptic hope, which the prophet relates to his nation, is extended in 2:28b-32a, where Joel states that "everyone who calls on the name of the Lord shall be saved" (v. 32a). The Pentecost speech by Peter (Acts 2:17b-21) recontextualizes this portion of Joel. In each case, the message is clear: Confession, true penance, and a sincere willingness to change can lead to new dispensations of God's grace.

Placed in a worship context, the challenge of Ash Wednesday is beautifully highlighted: Ashes in the face of troubling signs can lead us toward the wonders of a reconsecrated life in the Spirit. A plethora of signs exist today that suggest an advancing "plague of locusts"—a swarming plague that devours the poor, the abused, and the helpless in our midst, both in our nation and world. Perhaps too many of us today need to hear the "the ram's horn" (shofar) blown on Mount Zion as an urgent call to a solemn assembly to reassess a people's moral integrity and spiritual values. The problems of homelessness, drug abuse, violence, and gross materialism are everywhere evident. Far too many who call themselves Christian still so narrowly define religious obligations to the neighbor that many are estranged or moved to the periphery of our communities.

SECOND LESSON: 2 CORINTHIANS 5:20B—6:2

Paul, in this passage, lays forth the necessity for each person to be reconciled to (*katallasso*, "become friends with") God. The passage also highlights the usefulness of doing this immediately. No better time than the present moment is available to receive Christ's reconciliation to God.

The classic biblical texts on such friendship with God are as follows: "And he [Abraham] believed the Lord, and the Lord reckoned it to him as righteousness" (Gen. 15:6); and "thus the scripture [i.e., Gen. 15:6] was fulfilled that says, 'Abraham believed God, and it was reckoned to him as righteousness' " (James 2:23; see John 15:12). Abraham put complete faith and trust in God and acted accordingly, thereby his estrangement from God was removed. In 2 Cor. 5:18-19, Paul appeals to his readers to become friends with God; this is the leading criterion for authentic ministry and apostleship. Paul asserts that just as Abraham had responded in faith as a recipient of God's grace, Paul himself has sought to do likewise. (Abraham receives full treatment in the First Lesson, the Second Sunday in Lent.)

Paul has special reasons for arguing in this manner. In 1 Corinthians, the unity of the church is Paul's preoccupation; in 2 Corinthians, Paul himself is under attack on several fronts, including *ad hominem* arguments that disparage him personally (see 1:3-14; 2:1-10). Throughout the pastiche of epistolary fragments known as 2 Corinthians, Paul attempts valiantly to defend the integrity of his gospel, his apostolic office, and his own personhood against the charges brought by diverse and contentious opponents at Corinth.

In 2 Cor. 5:20b, Paul continues to express the theocentric core of his thought. He focuses not on what Jesus Christ has done, but on what God has done in the Christ-event (i.e., the death and resurrection). This saving event constitutes the basis of new possibilities for those who would be enemies of God; now instead they can become friends of God by virtue of accepting God's grace and by reexamining their priorities and values on the basis of this same grace.

Thus, Paul first asks his adversaries to be reconciled with God (v. 20). The implication is that they will then become friends (be reconciled) with Paul. The basis for Paul's request is verse 21: "For our sake [God] made [Christ] to be sin who knew no sin, so that in him we might become the righteousness of God." Jesus did not sin (see Heb. 2:14-18), and yet he was "made . . . to be sin" and was caught up in a web of sin ("For anyone hung on a tree is under God's curse" [Deut. 21:23]) for our sake. Paul's claim (v. 21b) is that God spared nothing in order to make persons (in this instance, Paul and his adversaries) show forth God's friendship in their lives as they work together with God (6:1a). In Paul's vision of the gospel, those who can only find fault in others have little opportunity to see or appreciate God's grace working its way in their lives. The actions of the adversaries are tragic signs (that is, sins) that God's grace seems extended to some in vain (6:1b).

Placed in a worship context, the texts from Paul reveal that he, no less than Joel, sees a community in crisis and seizes the moment to call even his adversaries to repentance—not to him, but before God— so that even this late hour may be transformed from a time of enmity to a day of salvation. Paul underscores the here and now by quoting Isaiah 49:8; he states: "See, now is the acceptable time; see, now is the day of salvation!" (2 Cor. 6:2).

As ministers of Christ's gospel, we need to be encouraged to see our public service as ministries of reconciliation. Through confession, penitential sacrifice, and an openness to change, we become friends with God and one another. The corporate executive, the carpenter, the police officer, the fast-food employee, the stockbroker, the drug addict seeking help, the factory worker, the distressed parent—we need this word now.

GOSPEL: MATTHEW 6:1-6, 16-21

The cultic law with its provisions for diverse public sacrifices and other duties is a hallmark of ancient Hebraic and subsequent Jewish religion. The Torah and later rabbinic texts reflect, in part, a concern for religious rituals performed in public. Some of these practices passed into Christian traditions, whether Coptic, Ethiopian, Orthodox, or Latin.

Toward the end of Matthew's Gospel, Jesus distinguishes between "the weightier matters of the law: justice and mercy and faith" and the other matters, such as tithing spices (Matt. 23:23). And throughout the Gospel, Jesus seems more concerned with mercy than with sacrifice: For example, Jesus says at the dinner table with tax collectors and sinners, "Go and learn what this means, 'I desire mercy, not sacrifice.' For I have come to call not the righteous but sinners" (Matt. 9:13; see Jos. 6:6); and when confronted concerning grain plucking on the Sabbath, Jesus repeats, "But if you had known what this means, 'I desire mercy and not sacrifice,' you would not have condemned the guiltless" (Matt. 12:7). In sum, Jesus centers on the ethical imperatives of love within society rather than on the community's piety and praise when this is separated from concern for mercy and justice.

Our passage is at the center of the Sermon on the Mount. These traditional teachings of Jesus were collected by the Gospel writer; it is unlikely that Jesus himself ever taught in such a sustained, disjointed manner. Also, Luke presents a similar set of sayings, usually called the Sermon on the Plain, as well as similar sayings throughout his Gospel; in contrast, many of these sayings are not mentioned in Mark or John. Thus, these sayings in Matthew likely have been stylized into a "mountain motif" (in Matthew, Jesus often is ascending or descending mountains) that enhances an emphasis on Jesus as the new Moses. Indeed, many scholars have suggested that this "higher righteousness" of the Matthean Jesus is addressed to both Jewish Christian legalists and antinomian Gentiles within Matthew's own divided community.

Three traditional Jewish religious obligations are selected in this lectionary text: almsgiving (vv. 2-4), prayer (vv. 5-6), and fasting (vv. 16-21). In the higher righteousness, these are to be practiced "in secret," a phrase used repeatedly (vv. 4, 6, 18) as a virtual critique of Jewish and Jewish Christian public displays of piety. Such public displays can become occasions for hypocrisy, and the term *hypocrisy* is common here and in Matthew 23.

Placed in a worship context, this Gospel passage seems odd, even counter to the practice of imposing ashes on the foreheads of worshipers, and Ash Wednesday can easily fall prey to such hypocritical displays of vacuous religiosity. Ash Wednesday worship is hollow if it leads people to a public display and little else.

The point of the text is to direct believers to the true intent of ritual piety: They are not to seek public approval or material rewards, but are to trust in God for the outcome of all actions. The point of this day is a changed mind, heart, and will redirected toward God and neighbor.

On the one hand, Matthew urges the reader to recognize that true piety or righteousness is primarily and finally a private matter, not an opportunity for pretense and superficiality; on the other hand, Joel and Paul provide a call to such true piety that is also public—returning to God means being reconciled to one another.

First Sunday in Lent

Lutheran	Roman Catholic	Episcopal	Common Lectionary
Gen. 2:7-9, 15-17, 3:1-7	Gen. 2:7-9, 3:1-7	Gen. 2:4b-9, 15-17, 25—3:7	Gen. 2:4b-9, 15-17, 25—3:7
Rom. 5:12, 17-19	Rom. 5:12-19	Rom. 5:12-19	Rom. 5:12-19
Matt. 4:1-11	Matt. 4:1-11	Matt. 4:1-11	Matt. 4:1-11

The Lenten sojourn of spiritual discipline is announced in the readings for this first Sunday. The theme of these passages is *imitatio Christi*— imitating Christ. When taken as a whole, these biblical texts usher listeners into a minidrama on the gift of paradise, on the tragedy of "paradise lost," and on the gift of paradise regained by taking seriously God's grace in the Christ-event. Here is the genuine basis for a renewed covenant buttressed by Jesus' own example and its implication: Go and do likewise.

The First Lesson (Gen. 2:4b—3:7) presents the mythopoetic image of pristine humanity in an original state of paradise. This idyllic existence, however, is soon destroyed because the humans seem unable to obey the divine imperative, "Do not eat. . . ." This inability is portrayed as the unwillingness to resist the devil's or evil's temptation to do other than God has commanded.

The Second Lesson (Rom. 5:12-19) is Paul's portrayal of the means by which believers can again have access to paradise. God through the Christ-event makes possible a "new Adam"—a new humanity that is faithful.

The Gospel (Matt. 4:1-11) sets forth the paradigm of Jesus as the model for faithful reentry into paradise. Matthew makes clear that just as Jesus resists the devil and his temptations, so Jesus' followers are to do the same. The temptation to evil may be always present for humans, but so is spiritual discipline that enables us, like Jesus, to put off doing those things that are unpleasing to God. Invitation and personal challenge, then, are the themes of this day.

FIRST LESSON: GENESIS 2:4B-9, 15-17; 2:25—3:7

This text and Romans 5 (see below) have caused much ink—and blood—to be spilled. Both texts have been enormously influential and often profoundly misunderstood. Gen. 2:4b opens the earlier of the two biblical accounts of creation. The verse is part of the Yahwist (J) account (Gen. 2:4b—3:24) that predates the Priestly (P) version of creation (Gen. 1:1—2:4a) by about five hundred years. The Yahwist's opening verse (2:4b) is itself a composite of still earlier African and Near Eastern myths that attempted to explain the divine origin of and intent for humanity and to account for the human tendency to become alienated from God.

The Yahwist's narrative can be understood as composed of two blocks. In the first block, Gen. 2:4b-25 relates the primal events of creation. This block has three units. The first unit (vv. 4b-9) indicates that the earth was created in one day (v. 4b) and that man was formed from the dust of the earth (v. 7), receiving the "breath of life" from God. Notice in this Yahwist version that no details are given for the creation of the other planets. Here, the human species is created even before vegetation, fish, or foul. One cannot but appreciate the distinctive purpose that God gives to the original man—"to till and keep" the earth (v. 15). This original divine purpose contrasts markedly with that stated in the Priestly version, which indicates that man is to "have dominion" over all the earth (Gen. 1:26). The later Priestly account has often been used to justify the complete domination and exploitation of our natural environment. In light of massive contemporary environmental problems, the ancient Yahwist reading has much to teach us, given its accentuation of preserving or keeping the earth as opposed to exploiting it.

The second unit of the first block (vv. 10-14), which reports a tenth-century B.C.E. perception of the location of the Garden of Eden, need not be dealt with at length. These verses too have been storm centers in scholarly circles, but suffice it to say that both Africa and Asia are indicated by two pairs of rivers: most probably the Blue and White Nile rivers in Africa and the Tigris and Euphrates rivers in the Near East.

The third unit (vv. 15-25) details the creation of a companion ("it is not good that the man should be alone" [v. 18]), one who is seen also as a "helper" or a "partner." From the time of the apostle Paul and the church fathers until today, this text has been used frequently to justify or even bolster the oppression and subordination of women.

In the second block, Gen. 3:1-24 is a story of crime and punishment that culminates in the expulsion of Adam and Eve from the Garden of Eden. That the text depicts Eve, the "helper," as actually a hindrance (3:1-7) has made the reading of Gen. 2:18 problematic for many persons today. Many persons have also tended to read aspects of this passage as calling for acquiescence to the "will of God" in the midst of pain and suffering because these are viewed as part of the continuing punishment for original sin (vv. 16-19).

A careful reading of these two blocks offers glimpses of often-overlooked features that can prove instructive and inspiring. Contemporary exegetes, notably Claus Westermann, observe that "man" in Genesis 2:7 means neither "male" nor the corporate humanity, but simply the human species (*adam* in Hebrew) "formed from the dust [*adamah*] of the ground." Again, the creation of the first human is complete only with three other steps: God needed to breathe "the breath of life" into it (v. 7), place it in the garden (v. 8), and then (vv. 22-25) differentiate it into male (*ish*) and female (*ishshah*). As Westermann notes, "The creation of woman completed the creation of humankind."

To be human, according to the Yahwist, means to be intrinsically related to God, to the remainder of creation, and to other humans. Being is communal, situated in the center of creation with the responsibility "to till it and keep it" (v. 15). These primeval bonds, these constitutive relationships, and their tragic fracture explain the human condition. In light of this, we can say that the passages describing the primal prohibition (vv. 15-17) and transgression (3:1-7) are not meant to narrate historical or quasi-historical events, but rather are meant to offer the reasons that suffering, shame, sin, and death have always been part of human existence.

A few words are in order, then, regarding "the tree of the knowledge of good and evil" (2:9) and the divine restriction attached to it (v. 17). One may wonder why God did not want human beings to have such knowledge. The surmise is theologically significant because God knows quite well that with such knowledge, people will tend to do evil precisely because it has the appearance of power apart from and yet rivaling God's power. One cannot but see aspects of this text amplified in Matt. 4:1-11 and Luke 4:1-14 (see below).

Placed in a worship context, the Yahwist text seems to indicate that the disobedience of Adam and Eve ruptures their erstwhile intimate relationship with God. Adam and Eve "fall" precisely because their actions represent an attempt to redefine their relationship with God. Yet God has already prescribed the terms of this relationship. It proves folly whenever human beings fail to understand this saving fact. The Yahwist thus sets the stage for a series of crime-and-punishment narratives that ultimately find resolution in the utter grace that God manifests in the Christ-event itself.

SECOND LESSON: ROMANS 5:12-19

Romans 5:12—8:39 is Part Two of Paul's epistle. The entire epistle is a working out of Romans 1:16: "For . . . the gospel . . . is the power of God for salvation to everyone who has faith, to the Jew first and also to the Greek." In Part One, "The Righteousness of God," Paul unfolds how a person through faith is righteous. In Part Two, he explicates in these "freedom chapters" how a person, righteous through faith, shall live. Here, the "power of God for salvation" means first that the believer is *freed from* God's wrath because the reign of grace is as wide as the reign of sin, and far more powerful (5:12-21). (For further discussion of Romans, see the sections below on the Second Lessons for the Second, Third, and Fifth Sundays of Lent.)

Both Adam and the notion of original sin feature prominently in Rom. 5:12-19 as Paul outlines the terms for believers to regain access to a paradise that was lost so long ago. It is startling that Paul's arguments are addressed not to unbelievers but to persons already associated with the church at Rome. The further surprise is that Paul rather audaciously addresses in such a forthright manner a church that he has never visited. His address to these Roman believers even has the tone of a theological testament, causing many interpreters to wonder about the exact occasion and purpose of this entire epistle. From Saint Augustine to Martin Luther, John Calvin, John Wesley, and Karl Barth, Romans has been regarded as an explosive and rather bold document that demands careful study. Some have gone as far as suggesting that in Romans, one encounters Paul as a systematic theologian. This assessment, however, is excessive because Paul here, as elsewhere in his letters, is at best a situational preacher merely attempting to demonstrate that the gospel, somewhat like the Torah, can be adapted to different living situations. Perhaps the genius of Romans is its demonstration that in this adaptability, the gospel supercedes even the Torah in offering a rich new prospect of freedom, new life, and a righteousness before God—the gospel brings believers to a fresh start in their Christian faith and life.

The historical setting and background of Romans are important. The Latin historian Suetonius in *Vita Claudia (The Life of Claudius)* reports on disturbances in Rome that involved "the Jews," resulting in the expulsion of Jews and evidently Jewish Christians (frequently confused with Jews because these Jewish Christians often retained various Jewish practices) in 49 C.E. The edict of Claudius Caesar Augustus Germanicus thus effectively disrupted and removed from Rome a fledgling Jewish Christianity that had been established there by missionaries not associated directly with Paul. Oddly enough, the young Emperor Nero, Claudius' successor, repealed the exile edict and enabled the church at Rome to reestablish itself in 54 C.E. This fact seems odd because a decade later this same Nero scapegoated the Christians when he burned Rome. Nevertheless, when Paul wrote the Epistle to the Romans, probably in 55 C.E. from Corinth, he was profoundly aware of the historic opportunity at once to introduce himself, to exert gently his own apostolic credentials, and to serve astutely as a reconciling mediator for a reorganizing church that needed to forge a more pluralistic identity because Gentiles were fully a part of this reorganized body. If this new experiment was to work without disturbance, then someone needed to outline a theological basis for Jews and Gentiles alike to claim afresh the gospel of God's righteousness. In Romans, Paul appoints himself to this task and skillfully undertakes it.

Romans 5:1—8:39 can be seen as the "freedom chapters," with these passages in Romans roughly paralleling a similar set of freedom chapters in Galatians. Whereas Romans 5–7 speaks of *freedom from* sin, death, and the Law, Galatians 3–4 speaks of *freedom from* varied "slave covenants." Likewise, Romans 8 identifies the constructive counterpart, an agenda of *freedom for* a new life in the Spirit, and Galatians 5 identifies an agenda of *freedom for* producing "the fruits of the Spirit." But in Galatians, Paul speaks to persons who are clearly backsliders, whereas in Romans, he addresses believers, implying strongly that they also need to wrestle afresh with the true repentance of conversion.

Ernst Käsemann, like many other New Testament exegetes who have examined Romans, separates Rom. 3:21—4:25 ("The Righteousness of God as the Righteousness of Faith") from Rom. 5:1—8:39 ("The Righteousness of Faith as the Reality of Eschatological Freedom"). Immediately prior to our reading, Paul in Rom. 5:1-11 introduces the new freedom passages. First, in 5:1-5, he traces the consequences of "justification by faith," utilizing the images of suffering and hope (vv. 2-5) in words eerily reminiscent of James 1:1-4. The idea that suffering produces hope alerts the reader to the simple fact that apparent adversity may be an opportunity to rely newly and exclusively on God and thereby recover the unique power of the Holy Spirit to make "a way out of no way." Second, 5:6-11 contrasts "suffering," "hope," and "love," as mentioned in vv. 2-5, with the statements "we were still weak" (v. 6), "we still were sinners" (v. 8), and "we were reconciled [and] . . . *will . . . be* saved" (v. 10; emphasis added). To understand how believers are justified and reconciled in Christ requires, in Paul's view, a radical reassessment of human weakness and proclivities for sin when apart from God's righteousness. The message was as cogent and apt for the ancient church at Rome as for modern churches struggling with the issue of multiculturalism and diversity today.

Romans 5:12-19 recalls the "original sin" of Adam and attempts to trace the consequences of that sin. Paul's aim is to contrast the old Adam and his "work" (sinful trespass) with the new Adam and his "work" (reconciling, justifying salvation). However much the Yahwist in Gen. 3:1-7 may have been thinking about the communal trespass of both Adam and Eve, Paul actually focuses on Adam as *man* in order to contrast him with the new "man" as God's new creation, namely, Jesus the Christ. Paul seems to place the responsibility for the first sin squarely on man as male, but by contrast challenges all believers to imitate the work of the new Adam who is a prototype not restricted to the particularity of gender. When Jesus of Nazareth becomes Jesus the Christ, the human gender recedes; behold the new has come (see 2 Cor. 6:2).

When placed in a worship context, the governing image of Rom. 5:15-17 is that of the "free gift" that is offered afresh, but now in Christ more abundantly. This is so because in the Garden of Eden the gift did not include the freedom to choose between good and evil (that knowledge was reserved); now both Jews and Gentiles have this possibility as a further testimony of God's utter righteousness.

To those who claim that we, like Adam and Eve, cannot fully predict what the outcome of our actions will be—that loving protection can easily slip into domination, for example—Paul sets forth two contrasting humanities. Thus, the prohibition not to eat fruit from the tree of the knowledge of good and evil in the garden (Gen. 2:17) is in no way reimposed here. Believers, in effect, have this knowledge through faith in Christ and now need to choose how it will be used in light of the gospel. The gates of paradise have now been reopened, defying the power of sin and death among believers. The Law (v. 20) certainly provided an interim access route, but Paul finds the Law incomparable to the free gift that God makes possible through a new humanity of obedience, Christ Jesus (v. 19).

GOSPEL: MATTHEW 4:1-11

The public ministry of Jesus follows his baptism and temptation (see Mark 1:12-13; Luke 4:1-14). In comparing the temptation narratives of Matthew and Luke, one should note the differences, such as the varied titles ascribed to the devil, the order and style of Old Testament citations, and the language that each uses. An important clue to Matthew's theme of the "higher righteousness" with decidedly moral overtones is already made clear. Jesus is baptized by the reluctant John: "Let it be so now; for it is proper for us in this way to fulfill all righteousness" (Matt. 3:15a). The way of higher righteousness is exemplified in Matthew's account of the temptations of Jesus (4:1-11). Unlike the repeated references to the Holy Spirit in Luke, the Matthean version indicates only that the Holy Spirit led Jesus into the wilderness to be tempted by the devil. It is as if Matthew places far more stress on Jesus' own ability to endure or resist the temptations without having to be sustained by another intermediary. In this way, Matthew introduces the element of *imitatio Christi* (imitating Christ) for his own highly divided community as well as for successive generations of Christian readers to the present.

The reference to a forty-day period of fasting "in the wilderness" recalls the parallel episodes of Moses' wilderness fast (Exod. 34:28; Deut. 9:9) and of Elijah (1 Kings 19:8). Matthew underscores the stark reality of the extended fast by indicating (v. 2) that following it, Jesus "was hungry." At the same time, however, Matthew highlights the humanity of Jesus (see Heb. 2:18). Each of the three temptations takes the form of stimulus-response or, better, point-counterpoint. The word *temptation* derives from the Greek verb *peirazo*, which, much like the

Hebrew term *massah*, usually means "to put to the test" and thus to tempt one to flunk the test.

The first temptation is the same in Matthew and Luke (and for all humanity) and involves the basic need for food. This need arises not only when one is deprived of sustenance but also when one undertakes the spiritual discipline of fasting. In this and the two succeeding temptations, the tempter introduces the temptation with the protasis ("if" clause) of a conditional sentence: "If you are the Son of God . . ." (Matt. 4:3). The challenge is clear because God's word from heaven— "This is my son, the Beloved, with whom I am well pleased" (3:17)— was evidently heard by the devil, too. Now, Jesus is confronted as to the validity of his identity as the Son of God, and the tempter uses food to entice Jesus not only to betray his calling but also to break his fast (cf. Gen. 25:29-34). Matthew 4:4 contains Jesus' response by way of Scripture (Deut. 8:3).

The second temptation in Matthew is the third one in Luke's parallel account. For Matthew, the more Jewish of the two Gospels, attention is turned to the pinnacle of the Temple in Jerusalem. In this scene (v. 5), the devil himself quotes Scripture (Ps. 91:11-12), seemingly taking Jesus' own lead from the former temptation. Because Matthew elsewhere repeatedly uses the title "son of David," it may be that the pinnacle of the Temple refers to the Tower of David. Notice how the devil repeats the challenge to Jesus' authority—"If you are the Son of God, throw yourself down" (4:5b). Here is the temptation to prove divine identity through magic or miraculous deed. Jesus' reply—"Do not put the Lord your God to the test" (v. 7b; a quotation from Deut. 6:16)—is a double entendre. If Jesus complied with this second request, then not only would the devil be putting God to the test but he would now also be putting God's son to the test. Jesus' response is a firm reaffirmation of the divine commission pronounced from heaven at his baptism.

The third and final test appears in Matt. 4:8-9 and constitutes the temptation of humanity to political power and influence. The modern reader should not miss the irony: The devil claims to possess such power ("authority") and the ability to transfer it ("all these things will I give you"). The insight is a chilling reminder of the many ways that political power has been severely abused in human history. This point requires care when examining New Testament passages such as Mark 12:13-17 (cf. Matt. 22:15-22; Luke 20:20-26) or Rom. 12:1-7, which take up the question of church-state relations. In any case, the devil uses the prospect of political might to attempt to seduce Jesus to change his loyalty from God to the demonic. Jesus, however, rejects outright any such offer; the offer is especially offensive when coupled with the command to "fall down and worship" the devil. With words that are biblically retrospective ("The Lord your God you shall fear; him you shall serve" [Deut. 6:13]) and prospective ("Worship God!" [Rev. 19:10]), Jesus continues to resist the devil who finally, in Matthew's version, gives up.

Placed in a worship context, the temptation narrative has a distinctive role in assisting persons today in their Lenten journeys. No text is so well suited to draw an analogy between Jesus' own struggle with demonic temptations and the necessary attitudes and spiritual disciplines needed by Christians similarly tempted. The *imitatio Christi* is implicit throughout the first five extended discourse sections that comprise the body of Matthew's Gospel.

Preachers may want to present these temptations as progressive: Each one takes place on higher ground and with a wider vista than its predecessor, until "all the kingdoms of the world" are at stake. This is a titanic battle of cosmic significance that ultimately confirms Jesus' messianic status by virtue of his obedience to God. Yet, over what are Jesus and the tempter fighting? The character of the temptations themselves can be seen as an elaboration of John the Baptist's message about the necessity for religious persons to repent and reorient their lives around God. In contrast with the Pharisees and Sadducees that John decries (Matt. 3:7-10), Jesus presumes nothing of God. The advent of the kingdom of heaven demands that we throw off religion as usual, which is characterized by

- *feeling good*: private complacency and self-absorption, a kind of religious self-gratification; the delusion is the thought that God has made one a special recipient;
- *feeling right*: self-righteousness and dogmatism; the delusion is that God has given one all the answers;
- *feeling secure*: authority and power; the delusion is that being religious gives one the right to dictate to others.

Although religion has different functions in contemporary North America from those in ancient Israel, still it is not difficult to see these same seductive self-delusions today. We too use religious observance as a means of private comfort and a goad to self-improvement, rather than as a serious challenge to our complacent life-style. We too are seduced by our religious certainties into thinking that we have the answers to difficult social and moral issues for everyone else in our family, church, and society. We too mistake religious pomp, status, privilege, and power for true worship and service of God (Matt. 4:10). Jesus himself provides the extraordinary example.

What Adam and Eve should have known, and what Jesus when confronted by the tempter knew better: God's promises are different from other promises; they are not meant to be cashed in materially. What is central and nonnegotiable in Christian faith is obedience to God. That involves a fundamental reorienting of our lives by centering them in their ultimate, divine context. In Christ's example, we glimpse the possibility of overcoming the profound alienation that is inherent in "paradise lost." During Lent, Matthew, like Paul, offers believers a fresh start in Jesus' illustration of how one achieves the higher righteousness after all.

Second Sunday in Lent

Lutheran	Roman Catholic	Episcopal	Common Lectionary
Gen. 12:1-8	Gen. 12:1-4a	Gen. 12:1-8	Gen. 12:1-4a (4b-8)
Rom. 4:1-5, 13-17	2 Tim. 1:8b-10	Rom. 4:1-5, 13-17	Rom. 4:1-5 (6-12), 13-17
John 4:5-26	Matt. 17:1-9	John 3:1-17	John 3:1-17 *or* Matt. 17:1-9

Biblical "call narratives" comprise the three passages selected for this Sunday. When such calls come, persons are often caught between the comfortably familiar and the terrifyingly new. Some, such as Abraham and Jesus, respond without hesitation; others, such as Nicodemus, seem overwhelmed. For those who seize or are seized by this call, the resulting faith is personal and at odds with the seeming reality. But each of these readings also emphasizes a communal dimension that should not be overlooked or ignored.

In the Old Testament passage, Gen. 12:1-8, God calls Abram (later Abraham) to go to a land (later revealed to him [v. 7]) and promises to make of him a great nation and a blessing to all peoples of the earth (v. 2). Abram responds in faith (v. 4a), despite his advanced age (he is seventy-five [v. 5]) and his childless marriage to Sarai (later Sarah).

In the New Testament Epistle, Rom. 4:1-17, Paul performs a clever midrash on the First Lesson and the prevailing understanding in the first century C.E. For centuries before Paul, the Jewish tradition (both in the Hebrew Bible, e.g., Isa. 19:24, and in the intertestamental period, notably in *The Book of Jubilees*) had revered Abram as a paradigm of righteousness. True, this tradition acknowledged Abram as the father of "the nations," but a distinctive claim was placed on him as the Hebrew patriarch. His universal significance was collapsed into ethnic particularity.

In the New Testament Gospel, either of two calls is present: in Matt. 17:1-9, Jesus' own call on the mount of transfiguration; or in John 3:1-17, the abortive call of Nicodemus to faith. In the transfiguration, Jesus is joined by Abraham and Moses and readily understands and reaffirms his call from God (Matt. 17:7).

In the nighttime visit, Nicodemus—a ruler of the Jews who speaks of "we" (John 3:1, 2)—has no comprehension, at least initially, of what Jesus means by suggesting that Nicodemus needs to be "born again," or literally to be "born from above" (John 3:3). The Samaritan woman in John 4 (see the New Testament Gospel, Third Sunday in Lent, below) is the exact opposite of Nicodemus; unlike him, she finds the wherewithal to respond "by faith." Nicodemus, in contrast, illustrates one whose situation is better than either Abraham's or the woman's but who, nevertheless, is caught between the familiar old and the unfamiliar new.

The preacher's task on this Sunday is to deliver such a "call narrative" to all with open ears to hear from the pulpit. Like Abram, Nicodemus, the disciples, many are taken by surprise with life's events—tragedies abound—even in technologically advanced, comfortable societies: career opportunities shift; health fails; resources dwindle; society becomes more violent and hateful. The call to faithfulness in God's promises offers the hope of renewed life in an unredeemed world.

FIRST LESSON: GENESIS 12:1-8

The "primeval history," or the first part of Genesis (1–11), forms one literary boundary for our text. This part makes use especially of the Yahwist (J, for Jahwist) source of the tenth century and of the Priestly (P) source of both exilic and postexilic traditions. Throughout this part, a crime-and-punishment motif (from J) can be noted (see chaps. 4, 9, 11) and an ascendancy motif (from P) can be seen in the genealogy of Gen. 11:10-27, 31-32, which explicitly establishes the rise of Shem among the sons of Noah.

The other boundary is Gen. 12:10—13:1, which narrates how Abram's interest in self-preservation places Sarai (and the promise) in jeopardy. The editorial theologizing of P is manifest as the stage is set for a new phase of salvation history. No longer is God's saving plan primarily reckoned in terms of crime and punishment. Now it is narrated in terms of *faith, obedience,* or lack thereof. Abram's extraordinary faith may have taken him first to Canaan, but his faith quickly received its first great test as Abram and Sarai had to sojourn even in "the land of Ham" (Ps. 105:23), namely, Egypt.

In Gen. 12:1-9, God issues a new call to Abram, evidently in Haran (still in the environs of Mesopotamia, or the Tigris and Euphrates river basin). Verses 1-3 are a classic "call narrative" wherein a divine revelation occurs that commissions an individual to change the course of his or her life and work. The text informs us that Abram receives such a mandate from God to leave his own country and simply go forth. The text does not offer any details on what sociological or psychological factors may have constituted a basis for Abram's decision to respond to this call. The reader is scarcely prepared to understand what qualified Abram to receive such a call in the first place. In fact, the call seems to come out of the blue. How did Abram know that it was God speaking? Had he experienced other divine revelations? After all, he was already seventy-five years old (v. 4)! Was Abram perceived by others as having lost his mind as a senile old man? The text answers only with silence.

Abram, we are told, simply responded (vv. 4-8) by stepping forth on faith alone, going forth "as the Lord had told him" (v. 4). He took his wife, Sarai, and even his nephew Lot (v. 5) as he courageously went forth *on trust* in a trustworthy God and *in faith* in a God who epitomizes faithfulness.

Placed in a worship context, this text alerts us to the surprising constituents to whom a call from God may come. Some individuals, who may never have thought about being beneficiaries and recipients of such calls, may need to hear about Abram's call narrative this Sunday. This passage, then, could be the basis for telling Abram and Sarai's story, although references to Acts 3:17-26, Rom. 4:1-24 (see below), and Hebrews 11 would likely need to be included.

Lent is a time for all Christians, including pastors, to reexamine their own call narratives. To what extent does one's call reflect a continued willingness to sojourn into unknown places "in faith" and completely "on trust" in God? God is constantly selecting seemingly insignificant individuals through divine calls and thereby offers them (us) opportunities for service of great significance like that of Abram, who, even though obscure, became the great patriarch for the nations.

SECOND LESSON: ROMANS 4:1-17

The entire Epistle to the Romans is a working out of Rom. 1:16-17: "For . . . the gospel . . . is the power of God for salvation to everyone who has faith, to the Jew first and also to the Greek," because whoever through faith is righteous shall live. In Part One, "The Righteousness of God" (1:18—5:11), Paul unfolds how a person through faith is righteous. In Part Two (5:12—8:39), he explicates in these "freedom chapters" how a person, righteous through faith, shall live. Thus, our passage—which explains that Abraham was justified by faith, not by works—provides key themes for Part Two.

Part One can be organized as follows. First, all are under God's wrath (1:18—3:20), both the unrighteous (1:18-32) and the righteous under the Law and circumcision (2:1—3:20). Second, the righteousness of God (3:21—5:11) is revealed through Christ (3:21-31) and witnessed to by the Law and the Prophets (4:1-25) so that we are saved from God's wrath by God's love (5:1-11).

Abraham was for Paul a crucial figure, and the promises of the Abrahamic covenant (Gen. 17:4-14; 22:15-18) were in Paul's mind as he worked out his understanding of what God had done in the Christ-event. Paul's vision of the risen Christ had forced him to a radical reevaluation of the purposes and promises of God, and of the possibility of redemption in a sinful world. The apostle thus centered his thoughts on four basic elements in the story of Abraham: (1) God promised Abraham and his descendants land, people, and blessing; (2) Abraham responded to his "call" *in faith*, and put his faith into practice through *obedience*; (3) God pronounced Abraham justified (Gen. 15:6, cited in Rom. 4:3—in Hebrew as well as in Greek, one word can mean "righteous" or "just," and another form of it "righteousness" or "justification"); and (4) this happened prior to the circumcision of Abraham (mentioned in Genesis 17, and thus subsequent to the "promises" and the pronouncement of righteousness [see Rom. 4:10]), that is, before Abraham could be said to have become a Jew.

Notice the way Paul wrestles with these ideas in Romans 4. He starts from the statement of Gen. 15:6, "[Abraham] believed the Lord; and the Lord reckoned it to him as righteousness [justification]." Abraham's departure from Haran was an act of faith (not a "work," which normally one associates with the Law). Paul viewed this as the grounds for Abraham's being "justified" (counted as righteous). Paul knew full well that his Jewish contemporaries (fully represented in Rome) read the texts of Genesis as the basis for the ideas of the promised land and the so-called chosenness of Israel. Paul, however, put the emphasis on Abraham's faith, asserting that trust in God, even on the part of one who does not necessarily have any unusual "works" to exhibit, is the basis for the imputation of righteousness. The conclusion is startling and provocative: God "justifies the ungodly" (Rom. 4:5a). No stronger expression could be given of the Christian conviction. Whoever responds to God's call in faith is never beyond the possibility of redemption. God can liberate any of us from the constraints of our past.

Paul's argument seems to be based on the following correspondences of terms and concepts:

- *Promise of land:* Paul formulates this as meaning to "inherit the world" (Rom. 4:13). Paul's wording recalls numerous Old Testament references to the inheriting of the land (or earth), which are reminiscent also of Jesus' word that the meek will "inherit the earth" (Matt. 5:5). In Paul, the words have an eschatological ring and are apparently aimed at the idea of ultimate redemption (see Rom. 8:16-23).

- *Descendants:* Paul is sensitive to his own Jewish descent and the prevailing high esteem accorded Abraham in the intertestamental Jewish literature. He calls Abraham "our ancestor according to the flesh" (Rom. 4:1). His new emphasis, however, is that Abraham is the "ancestor of all who believe," whether circumcised or not (Rom. 4:11-12), contravening Gen. 17:14. A shift in the understanding of this promise is noticeable on Paul's part in comparison to the text of Genesis 12. In Genesis, Abraham is promised that from him would come a multitude of descendants. Paul nuances the matter differently by asserting that Abraham's descendants are the recipients of God's promises, and he occupies himself therefore with the question of the *identity* of Abraham's descendants. In Paul's midrash, Abraham's descendants are those who have faith like that of Abraham. In short, "descendants" in Genesis 12 constitute one of the promises to Abraham; by contrast, Paul reinterprets texts such as Gen. 22:18 to mean that any of the nations that believe are the *recipients* of the promises and descendants of Abraham (see Gal. 3:29).

- *The blessing:* In Genesis the term *blessing* may refer only to Abraham's monotheism (note also the monotheistic revolution of Pharaoh Akenaton). The term *promise* for Paul, in contrast, refers to God's bestowal of righteousness on all who have faith; this use of the term *promise* (*epangelia*) appears to be a Pauline innovation because it is not used in this way in any prior Jewish text (traditionally, the term only meant "consent," or "decision").

Placed in a worship context, this text from Paul has frequently baffled Christians. Even in the early second century, the author of 2 Peter 3:15b-16 remarks on how confusing Paul's words seem to be at times. Moreover, his thought can scarcely be reduced to a theological system. The premises of his thought are so radical and his arguments so intricate (even at times seemingly inconsistent) that many Christians find it difficult to comprehend all that he had to say.

Nevertheless, Paul's vision of God's purpose has offered countless persons hope in the face of hopelessness (in contrast to optimism; see the New Testament Epistle, the Third Sunday in Lent), the secure basis for a new beginning, and freedom from bondage to the past. Paul expresses the reality of God's justifying grace as the bringing of life out of death: "God . . . gives life to the dead and calls into existence the things that do not exist" (Rom. 4:17). And his use of Abraham as the exemplar of faith called into existence by God in an otherwise dead body and cul-de-sac situation might give a preacher a helpful approach for addressing believers anew with God's call in their lives. Just as Abraham's faithful response to God's call enabled him to start afresh, Paul sees a similar pattern not only in salvation history given in the Christ-event but also in his own life just as we might see this pattern in ours.

GOSPEL: JOHN 3:1-17

(For John 4:5-26, see the Third Sunday in Lent.)

Characters in the Gospel of John are most deliberately depicted. Each one exemplifies a clearly delineated point of view and communicates an aspect of Johannine theology. John's Gospel is based on the distinction between the world *(kosmos)*, on the one hand, created by God and yet now a realm in which we live in ignorance, falsehood, flesh, and bondage, and the heavenly "things," on the other hand (see John 3:12).

Jesus is now the Christ of glory who embodies as Logos the presence of God, characterized by truth, light, life, spirit, knowledge, and freedom. In contrast to the Synoptic Gospels, Jesus' teachings in John do not seek to prove Jesus' true identity; rather hearers and readers alike are asked only to accept or reject his sonship as fact. This request is made without reference to repentance—so familiar in Matthew, Mark, and Luke—and, apart from this passage (vv. 3, 5), without reference to the kingdom of God. Jesus' teaching in John, moreover, centers on his own divine status; hence the well-known "I am" sayings are more abundant than in the Synoptics.

In John 3, Nicodemus functions as a person who is favorably attracted to Jesus, but who is strategically (intentionally?) puzzled by what he takes to be otherworldly allusions in Jesus' words. Although Nicodemus is impressed by Jesus' teachings as well as by his deeds ("signs" [v. 2]), he is not a disciple. His final words are, "How can these things be?" (v. 9). One needs to remember that Nicodemus has all of the conventional trappings of worldly status, which the Samaritan woman (Third Sunday in Lent) lacks.

The two figures in the narrative are described as "teachers" (Nicodemus, a "teacher of Israel" [v. 10]; Jesus, "a teacher who has come from God" [v. 2]). Nicodemus is described further as "a Pharisee," "a leader of the Jews," and as one who is familiar with Jewish traditions ("signs") and terms, such as "kingdom of God" and "Rabbi" (vv. 1, 2, 3). He has heard impressive things about Jesus, describing him as "a teacher . . . from God" and one in whom the presence of God accomplishes "signs." Yet, like the rich young ruler of the Synoptics (Matt. 19:16-30; Mark 10:17-31; Luke 18:18-30), Nicodemus seems simply too attached to worldly or "earthly things" to apprehend "heavenly things"—calls or opportunities for new life, new beginnings. Jesus speaks here on the level of ultimate reality while Nicodemus responds with puzzlement. From the outset, however, Nicodemus protects himself from loss (i.e., "hedges his bet") by approaching Jesus "by night" (v. 2)—a time when few, if any, would see his approach and thereby hold him accountable for such action.

Still the conversation between Jesus and Nicodemus centers on the possibility (and necessity) of new birth, a birth "from above" (the double meaning of the Greek expression defies exact duplication in English). Jesus speaks of a new orientation of life based upon "heavenly things" (v. 12), that is, those things in the realm of spirit, truth, light, knowledge, and freedom. This birth, this new orientation, is also presented as essential for seeing the kingdom of God (v. 3). One might say that the glimpse of the transcendence experienced by Peter, James, and John in the Synoptics' account of the transfiguration (an account absent from the Gospel of John) is here set forth as an essential aspect of true life.

The aftermath of the narrative (vv. 11-17), which culminates in the motif of condemnation and salvation, confirms the function of the Nicodemus episode: A person who is attracted to the Truth and his newness, but who remains scarcely prepared to accept the terms of this new adventure, misses out on the new life. Jesus states that the Son of man needed to descend from heaven because otherwise no one would be aware of these heavenly things (vv. 12-13). But this awareness is communicated by the Son of man's being lifted up on a cross—just as Moses put up the bronze serpent in the wilderness (Num. 21:4-9). In that text, the people were grumbling about their trip through the wilderness and their care (the reality of death, the "lack of water," and "this worthless food" [v. 5]). God sent fiery serpents among the people so that many died. Then they cried out to Moses that they had sinned by having spoken against Moses and God, and they beseeched Moses to pray for them. Then God commanded Moses to post a bronze serpent so that those who were bitten and looked on it should live. In just such a manner, Jesus has come to be posted so that people will view the heavenly things and be rescued.

This allusion to Numbers 21 sets up one of the most-beloved statements of the Bible for many Christians (John 3:16). The astounding nature of this verse can be missed if the context of Nicodemus' reticence to understand heavenly things, the bronze serpent's offer of life, or the function of the term *world* are forgotten. The "world," as in several other religions of the time, is a realm of human existence, and it is marked by several negative attributes: transitoriness, falsehood, blindness, ignorance, bondage, and death. For many non-Jewish intellectuals of the time, this world is not the locus of redemption; in fact, it was considered the sphere from which humans needed to be redeemed. In much Jewish eschatology, a corresponding contrast between the present age and the ages to come was common. Therefore, when John asserts that God "loved the world," it is probably intended as a paradox and an intellectual affront. This world, subject to change and decay and death, is nevertheless loved by God, and the evidence for this love is that God will yield up the only Son. This "love" is the present hope and basis for the world and even Nicodemus to change or be born anew and live a new life in the Spirit.

In spite of the astounding statement in John 3:16, however, this passage does not communicate the wholeness of the Christian faith and life. We find in it no direction for ordering our earthly life, no ethical maxims such as Jesus gives in the Synoptics—but simply an assertion of faith (God gave God's Son) that leads to eternal life. This verse, a call to faith, should not be taken in isolation from all that John later says in chapter 13 about the law of love. Nor can it be a substitute for the insights of Paul and for the other this-worldly concerns depicted in the work of Jesus in the other Gospels.

Placed in a worship context, this text calls to mind Dante's definition of hell as the condition of eternally remaining what one is. Little that we encounter in this life can be more destructive of the human spirit than the feeling that things will always be as they are now.

John portrays Nicodemus as one who is a searcher for truth and a religious-political leader. In a time in which we are accustomed to political manipulation and cynicism, when we are taken aback if we should witness an act of personal integrity—truth itself has become a scarce commodity. A life without integrity, however, is ephemeral, broken. Jesus offers new birth to broken lives, a newness that is ever received, lifting our sights to the truth that lies beyond the confines of our own small worlds.

Many seek a divine call as the opportunity for a new beginning—indeed, a new life. In the midst of the death and despair, glimpses of the transcendent break through. The preacher's task is to deliver the call to faith anew: Nicodemus (and Betty and David and Delores and George . . .) "the wind blows where it chooses, and you hear the sound of it, but you do not know where it comes from or where it goes. So it is with everyone who is born of the Spirit," and today the Spirit blows here for you.

ALTERNATIVE GOSPEL: MATTHEW 17:1-9

The Matthean account of Jesus' transfiguration—when seen as a reaffirmation of his call in Matt. 3:17—interrupts the traditional Lenten themes of penitence and self-sacrifice. It also points forward as an eruption of divine glory in the course of Jesus' Galilean ministry that anticipates his resurrection. The pivotal position of the narrative in the outline of the Synoptic Gospels (Matthew, Mark, and Luke) needs to be noted. In this light, the transfiguration can be understood as an account of new beginnings—and one of startling proportions.

In the Synoptics, the narrative of Jesus' transfiguration (see Mark 9:2-8; Luke 9:28-36) is linked with that of Peter's confession (Matt. 16:13-16; see also 17:1). The two constitute the great turning point of the entire ministry of Jesus. Although these two narratives bristle with difficult and controverted details, a few things stand out as foundational. Prior to these narratives:

- Very few individuals had raised the possibility of Jesus' messiahship or of his divine sonship (the exceptions are Matt. 8:28; Mark 5:1-43; Luke 8:26-30). The question of public opinion—"Who do people say that I am?" (Matt. 16:13-14)—produced diverse responses: John the Baptist, Elijah, Jeremiah, or one of the prophets. At a time of apocalyptic expectancy, Palestinian Jews were awaiting the return or rebirth of any number of the prophets as a sign of the messianic age. But Peter's response to the next question ("Who do you say that I am?") introjects something radically new into the Synoptic account: The disciples need to decide for themselves once and for all!

- Jesus had alluded to the possibility of a violent end for himself, but here for the first time he explicitly states that he "must go to Jerusalem and undergo great sufferings . . . and be killed, and on the third day be raised" (Matt. 16:21). This is the first of the so-called passion predictions. From this point the idea of Jesus' impending death more or less replaces the motif of the kingdom of God (kingdom of heaven) as the subject of Jesus' own utterances.

In the narrative of the transfiguration, which follows immediately that of Peter's confession and is linked to it by the mention of "six days" in Matt. 17:1, this new turn in the ministry of Jesus receives divine confirmation by means of the heavenly voice (known in the Jewish tradition as the *bath qol*, the "daughter of the voice"), already heard in Matt. 3:17.

What is this new turn, this new beginning? The answer is found when we consider the function of Moses and Elijah in this narrative. Moses and Elijah had several things in common. For example:

- Both were interpreted in Jewish tradition as having been translated into heaven without experiencing death (this was believed about

Moses on the basis of the statement in Deut. 34:6 that the location of his grave was not known, and about Elijah by virtue of the description of his assumption into heaven in 2 Kings 2:1-25). Because they experienced the presence of God prior to the resurrection, they both were quite appropriate for a narrative such as this, one that involved earlier prophets who were called by divine proclamations.

- Both lived at a critical, survival-threatening juncture in Israel's history. Moses was the pivotal figure in the birth of the nation of Israel, and Elijah was the fearless spokesman of Yahweh during the hegemony of Baal worship (the Phoenician-Canaanite religion).

- Both became prototypes of the category of prophet. Around Elijah there grew a mass of legends, including that regarding his function as precursor of the end times (see Mal. 4:5), and Moses also became the prototype of the final prophet (see Deut. 18:18).

- Most important: The two together came to represent and typify in a shorthand manner the two dominant traditions of the Israelite religion, namely, the Law and the Prophets—the two major sections of the Hebrew Scripture that had reached canonical status by the time of the New Testament writers. Moses and Elijah thus represented the religion of Israel, that is, Judaism. The Christian story of Jesus' transfiguration—found only in the Synoptics—is one of the few in the Synoptics that centers on the *person* of Jesus in contrast to his *teachings* or his *actions*. Our text, then, is one early charter for the Christian doctrine of Jesus the Christ.

In the narrative, Peter, James, and John are amazed to see Jesus conversing with Moses and Elijah as a peer. This is expressed by Peter's rather crude suggestion to build three booths (tents) to commemorate the astounding event (Matt. 17:4). The divine voice, however, breaks through this level of thought with a now-familiar, authoritative proclamation: *"This* is my Son, the Beloved; . . . , listen to *him!"* (v. 5; emphasis added). The voice thereby asserts in this context not the equality of Jesus with the Law and the Prophets but his superiority over them. The point is emphasized again by the statement that the three disciples looked up and "saw no one except Jesus himself alone" (v. 8).

Placed in a worship context, this passage presents Jesus' supreme authority, which permeates the Gospels and the New Testament as a whole. This distinctive aspect of Christian piety provides divine sanction and further approval of the radically new beginning represented by Jesus' call and his identity as announced in Peter's confession (16:16) and in Jesus' own disclosures (16:17-21, 24-28).

Again, this Sunday's First Lesson is a counterpoint to Jesus' ministry. Whereas Abraham and Sarah set out to a new country, and whereas Abraham would become a blessing to all the world's families by virtue of his passionate faith in and obedience to God, Jesus set out for Jerusalem to become the exemplar of redemptive self-giving through whom, Christians believe, all the world's families can share in the blessings vouchsafed in the descendants of Abraham.

Third Sunday in Lent

Lutheran	Roman Catholic	Episcopal	Common Lectionary
Isa. 42:14-21	Exod. 17:3-7	Exod. 17:1-7	Exod. 17:3-7
Eph. 5:8-14	Rom. 5:1-2, 5-8	Rom. 5:1-11	Rom. 5:1-11
John 9:1-41	John 4:5-42	John 4:5-26, 39-42	John 4:5-26 (27-42)

With the Third Sunday in Lent, we come to an approximate midway point in this season of penitence and sacrifice. By this time persons who have chosen to practice Lenten spiritual disciplines may either feel settled and comfortable in their sacrifices or be anxious for Easter to arrive so that they can resume their usual routines. Many may be restless with a season that seems only to become gloomier with each passing Sunday, as we walk with Jesus toward his inevitable crucifixion. Whatever attitude may be most prevalent in the minds of churchgoers during these days, the lessons for this Sunday are fortuitous because they speak to both the troubled and the satisfied.

Whereas on the first two Sundays of Lent the focus of the text was on the origins of human sin and the work of God in history, on this Sunday we focus on the faithfulness of God to all who are in need. Yet this emphasis is not all individualistic; these texts also speak of God's relationship to those in right relations with others, that is, in community. In each lesson humankind is claimed as God's own. From the gift of water at Massah and Meribah (Exod. 17:1-7) to the living water given to the Samaritan woman (John 4:5-42) to the pouring out of the Holy Spirit for our benefit, the preacher has many opportunities this Sunday to exhort listeners to drink from new fountains of water and to revitalize spiritual discipline at this pivotal stage in the Lenten journey.

FIRST LESSON: EXODUS 17:1-7

Unlike the Epistle or Gospel lessons, the Old Testament text for today has only an indirect antecedent in the pericopes of the other Lenten Sundays. In Exod. 17:2c, Moses asks the thirsty Israelites, "Why put the Lord to the test?" Then in verse 7, God (like Jesus in Matt. 4:1-11) demonstrates that no such test is necessary. In any event, we need to consider the larger literary context for our reading in Exodus. This should be profitable to both the preacher and the listener. Exodus 15 contains the well-known story of the miraculous passage of Israel through the Sea of Reeds. In Exodus 16, the people of Israel are near starvation in the wilderness of Sinai and complain yet again to Moses. As a test of obedience, the Lord sends upon them manna and quail, with explicit instructions on the manner in which each is to be gathered.

The complaints of today's text, therefore, are not isolated incidents; as the text is presented, they fall hard on the heels of a series of miraculous incidents in which the Lord provides for the safety and sustenance of God's people. Here the Israelites have come to Rephidim, where they find themselves without water. They "quarrel" (Heb.: *riv*) with Moses. In Hebrew, this word has the sense of a complaint between two parties that must be resolved by an outside arbitrator. Yet their complaint is not just with Moses; by extension, it is also with God. The water that they demand is not at Moses' command to give. Moses obviously is frustrated by a people who have such short-term memories when the faithfulness of God is concerned: "Why do you test the Lord?" (v. 2). In verse 4, when he calls upon God, he can not bring himself to claim them as his own, much less as belonging to God—they are *this* people. They are to him unrecognizable, or worse, an enemy, because they threaten even to stone Moses to death (v. 46).

The ungrateful, forgetful Israelites may provoke our scorn, but we should not forget that their complaint is not entirely unwarranted. They need water (see Exod. 15:22-25). Their complaining may grate on us, but they are not being unreasonable. Freedom from oppression is not a guarantee of happiness or prosperity, as the turmoil following the breakup of the Soviet Union in 1991 and the urban riots and uprisings following the 1992 Rodney King verdict in Simi Valley so aptly demonstrate. When the faces of hunger, thirst, and other woes loom large—and these are far too common—the face of God must indeed seem dim to the victims. Criticizing a visible leader is much more immediately satisfying than directing complaints to an invisible deity. Are we not just as likely today to resist those who cry out in need? Consider only the increasing plight of the homeless throughout America in the early 1990s. We may resent the pleas of these complainers and refuse to recognize them as fellow human beings, much less as children of God. Are we any more inclined than was Moses to call out to God on their behalf?

The rest of our text shows that God is far less bothered by the complaints of the people of Israel than either Moses or ourselves. God does not rebuke them or criticize Moses, but rather directs Moses to take several of the leaders and to meet God at the rock at Horeb (v. 6a). There God instructs Moses to strike the rock with his staff—as earlier he had struck the Nile River in Africa—and water is brought forth. This place therefore is named Massah ("to put to the test") and Meribah ("to quarrel or contend") because of the *riv* that took place here—a test, although unnecessary, acknowledged and completed by God.

In this dispute, however, God acts as both a party (indirectly) and as an arbitrator. We see a God who impartially acts on behalf of Israel, even in the face of their forgetfulness and unfaithfulness. Israel may not remember God's great acts on their behalf, but God does. God still lays claim to them. The Lord is the one who has brought them to this point and does not intend for them to die. The Lord will settle this dispute and use the obedience of Moses to set things right.

Understandably, for some on the Lenten journey the pressures of spiritual discipline are weighing heavily by the Third Sunday. We are reminded by this passage that God still guides us on our journey. Just as God led Israel to Rephidim, so also does God set us on our way. Our Lenten sacrifices are meager compared to the woes of Israel in the wilderness and the sacrifices of countless others who endured much hardship through faith (Hebrews 11). Some in our midst struggle to find just the essentials for daily living, much less make a Lenten sacrifice of some non-necessity. Yet we still complain. This text can remind us all that God is not only faithful to meet us in our essential need, but also that God is able to bear the brunt of our complaint without vindictiveness or wrath. (Would that most pastors could live up to that standard under the murmuring of irate parishioners—even Moses had problems doing so!)

Most importantly, those who preach this text can remind those who hear it that God is always present for the community of the faithful, and is binding us together in our obedience as well. Those who are bearing the weight of loss, absence, or sacrifice are met together by God. They are in our midst—not only next to us in the pew, but also with us in spirit. The preacher may do well to raise the question that closes verse 7 ("Is the Lord among us or not?") and demonstrate that the presence of God is indeed with those who are in need and, though we may see them only on television or other mass media, those in need are with us as well, bidding us to share the sustenance of God that has been given to us.

ALTERNATIVE FIRST LESSON: ISAIAH 42:14-21

This text, which appears only in the Lutheran lectionary for the Third Sunday in Lent, is nevertheless worthy of wider study. Isaiah 42 begins the first in a series of "Servant Songs" that featured prominently in early Christian literature as Jesus himself was interpreted often as the preeminent suffering servant (a distinguishing feature in Mark's Gospel and the basis of Philip's hermeneutic of Isa. 53:7-8 in Acts 8:26-40). Our passage relieves the reader from the penchant of premature celebrations of "cheap grace"! Here one needs to cope in a sober way with the reality of God's severe judgment against those who test even the patience of God, thereby subverting their election to a life of divine service in the way of righteous living. In an uncanny manner, Isa. 42:14-21 reminds us all that even in the midst of "captivity" (diverse literal and metaphorical states of bondage), we are still held accountable for the quality of life that we choose to live.

As to the wider literary context of the reading, we should note that the so-called Deutero-Isaiah wrote during the sixth century B.C.E. during the Babylonian Captivity. Many of the Jewish exiles in Babylon transformed their lament about "missed opportunities" in Zion (Ps. 137:1-4) into constructive and responsible actions (Jer. 29:1-32). This became the righteous remnant, and, in Isa. 42:1-4, they are those who inspire such words as, "Here is my servant, whom I uphold, my chosen, in whom my soul delights; I have put my spirit upon him; he will bring forth justice to the nations." But there are others who, according to Isa. 42:14, have continued only to lament, grumble, and, worse, lose faith in God completely; these are the ones who fall under judgment through the passage.

In Isa. 42:14-21 the judgment against the faithless and others of limited vision is stark and graphic. The text identifies harsh punishments that are about to be meted out: "I will lay waste mountains and hills" (v. 15a); "I will turn the rivers into islands" (v. 15b); "I will lead the blind by a road they do not know" (v. 16a); "I will turn the darkness before them into light" (v. 16c); and so forth. The specter of doom is held out for the disobedient and weak in resolve who have acquiesced to other gods (v. 17c). Deutero-Isaiah addresses this part of the nation in bondage as if they had truly become "deaf" and "blind" to all the saving acts that God had performed for them in the past. They are those who have a "record" (literally, "the Law," but here as a record of past saving acts) of divine intervention on their behalf; and yet this seems not to have mattered.

Like a few other biblical texts, this one has a stunning message for churchgoers in the context of our Lenten journey: Despite the hard times imposed by a faltering political economy, we dare not forget the plethora of past saving acts on our behalf made possible by God. Lent is also a time for such remembrance, lest unwittingly we too abandon spiritual and moral values in order to survive by any means possible. Setbacks—whether only temporary or genuinely threatening to one's career, family, or life—should never be the cause to abandon's one faith. On the contrary, in the wilderness experiences of life, God acts to encounter us anew.

SECOND LESSON: ROMANS 5:1-11

(For Eph. 5:8-14, see the Fourth Sunday in Lent.)

In the section on the Second Lesson for the Second Sunday in Lent, Part One of Romans was outlined. To recall: The righteousness of God (3:21—5:11) is revealed through Christ (3:21-31) and witnessed to by the Law and the Prophets (4:1-25) so that we are saved from God's wrath by God's love (5:1-11). Several comments regarding Pauline terminology from that Sunday will also apply here.

"In the entire Scripture there is scarcely another text like this chapter, scarcely one so expressive." So Martin Luther described this chapter of Romans, and indeed, preachers may find themselves daunted by the prospect of preaching on these verses that may well represent the theological highpoint of the apostle Paul, if not all of Scripture. They are so well known and so often commented on that one may be reluctant to add to what we have already said in the Second Lesson for the First Sunday in Lent. Indeed, the very familiarity of these verses may easily tempt us to misinterpretation; this lesson deserves continued meditation and study.

As with the Old Testament lesson, a dispute is involved here, although it is not stated explicitly. "We have peace with God" assumes that some quarrel has existed that has now been or should now be settled. The peace that Paul writes about here is not simply a sense of inner well-being and satisfaction (although this may well be a fruit of this peace). On the one hand, the peace being referred to may involve being in a right relationship with another, in this case, peace between humans and God. On the other hand, this peace may refer to the situation that should obtain in the reorganizing church at Rome. God has set the terms for this peace: Jew and Gentile justified by faith, faith that is a gift of God. Paul envisions a peace with God that is through Jesus Christ. Both Christ and faith are necessary for this justification that brings us into peace with God. Relying only on faith apart from Christ leads us to the error of trusting in our own faculties and merits, not in those of Christ. Relying on Christ apart from faith leads to the error of not demonstrating faith through works of righteousness. Faith and righteous deeds are inseparable in the mind of the apostle.

Lest we fall into the pit of works-righteousness (self-appointed deeds undertaken apart from faith in Christ), however, we need to remember that faith is a gift of grace expressed in works. (Here Paul and the Epistle of James [2:14-26] are much closer than is often acknowledged.) In Paul's view, Christ gains for us access to this grace. This accessed grace does not leave us in a static condition or stuck in one place, but launches us forward into the future, a future that is marked by sharing in the glory of God (v. 2; cf. 3:23). Our peace with God does not mean that suffering will not come our way, but we can be assured that this suffering will strengthen the faith that seals our justification, and thus lead us to the fulfillment of the hope that God promises us— sharing in God's glory (vv. 3-4).

Hope, of course, is the bridge between faith and love (cf. 1 Cor. 13:13) and points us forward to a future reality that has implications for the present. For this reason we are able to boast now of our share in God's glory. Hope, then, needs to be distinguished from optimism, a belief that the future will be better than the past. Here hope is lost because individuals believe that history is on their side. Hope also needs to be distinguished from various forms of nostalgia, a belief that the past can once again replace the present. Again, hope is displaced by a sense of history. Instead, hope is the deep-seated conviction that in spite of the present evils and oppressions, justice will still be accomplished.

It may seem strange to hear a text that so explicitly speaks of "boasting" (vv. 2-3, 11) in the middle of a season in which we are supposed to seek humility, but Paul is making a natural theological progression here. According to Ernst Käsemann, *Commentary on Romans* (Grand Rapids, Mich.: Eerdmans, 1980), "It is presupposed that boasting is an existential factor in human existence, namely, an expression of human dignity and freedom. . . . If as Paul sees it existence is defined by its Lord, the basic understanding of existence comes to expression in boasting. In this a person tells to whom he belongs" (133).

From the start to this text in the Epistle to the Romans, Paul has been doing precisely this—establishing to whom we belong, announcing God's decision of our justification by faith (Rom. 3:28). In justifying us, God also establishes ownership of us. Boasting is therefore an expression of the faith by which we are justified. Apart from faith, apart from Christ, our existence loses its definition and we boast fruitlessly of false images in which we establish ourselves. Justification restores our true image in God and, consequently, that human dignity and freedom of which Käsemann writes.

The rest of the text reinforces this view. All this has been set into motion by the love of God for humankind, a love that is not effected by human action, but a love that is itself God's nature. God's nature is shown to us by concrete action—giving Christ to die for us. As at Massah and Meribah (Exodus 17), God's love is proven to us. In our Old Testament lesson the people of Israel put God to the proof; here Paul tells us that God proves God's self. God arbitrates the dispute between the divine and humankind through the giving of self—the self as represented in Jesus. In doing so, the love of God is poured out to us by the Holy Spirit, just as the waters of life were poured out to the people at Meribah and Massah.

By this action, not only is our hostility toward God removed, but we are saved from God's wrath as well. God's love for humankind does not preclude this wrath, this righteous indignation over our disobedience and sin. The death of God's Son "reconciles" (the Greek term means "make friends with") us to God and brings us to peace. Being reconciled, we are given a future and a hope in which we need not fear the wrath of God.

Throughout these verses, Paul consistently uses the first person plural: "*We* are justified"; "*we* are saved"; "while *we* were still weak"; "God proves his love for *us*"; "Christ died for *us*"; and so forth. Modern-day Christians too readily find comfort in these verses regarding their own personal salvation (and certainly Martin Luther did so himself). Caution is advised, however, because we need to consider the communal, universal aspects of Paul's thought. We can not reduce this to the narrow, selfish categories of "I'm OK; you're OK" or the other models of individualistic self-aggrandizement. Paul sees Christ's justifying action as restoring the image of the community. Paul's conviction that Jesus Christ is our only access to peace with God is highly focused. For him, it is clear that this action on God's part is on behalf of broad constituencies. God's love not only saves and justifies individuals but also formulates and emboldens the community. This salvation is for everyone!

At this midpoint of Lent, it is refreshing to hear that our own efforts and disciplines are insufficient in themselves to reconcile us to God. Rather, God's own saving act in the death-resurrection and sacrificial life of Christ brings us into that right relationship. Our sacrifice is but a pale reminder of what was done for us by the love of God. Those who would boast of their own temporary sacrifices are brought up short by the words of Paul—it is Christ alone in whom we should boast. Those who find dignity and freedom to be but hackneyed words of false hope are restored—God's grace gives us our true identity. Sublime promises such as these can renew and strengthen us for our Lenten journey. As a result, each of us can better share in the kingdom and return of Christ that yet awaits us. We live between the *already* of what God has done in Christ and the *not yet* of what God still wants to do with us and all creation.

GOSPEL: JOHN 4:5-42

(For John 9:1-41, see the Fourth Sunday in Lent.)

Today's Gospel lesson is the longest pericope in the New Testament. It is the second part of the Nicodemus episode; an intentional contrast, undoubtedly, its message is vital to displaying the Gospel writer's overall theology. A number of surprises emerge: Jesus the Jew, in requesting water from the woman, transcends the prohibition that Jews and Samaritans are to have no social intercourse (vv. 7-9); Jesus the man publicly acknowledges her full humanity as a woman; Jesus as the Christ of Glory sees beyond her many faults to find her need and thereby to transform her completely.

As the scene begins, Jesus is tired and thirsty; he asks the Samaritan woman for a drink. John explains the scandal of this situation by saying that "Jews do not share things in common with Samaritans" (v. 9). But the problem of Jesus' behavior goes even deeper: Not only was it considered improper for a man to approach a strange woman and engage her in conversation, but for a Jew to approach a Samaritan woman was doubly risky, because in so doing he risked being considered unclean. Jews thought of Samaritan women as being in a perpetual state of uncleanliness, as if they were constantly menstruating; to come into contact with such a woman would render one impure. The woman recognizes the unusual nature of the situation and at first indignantly challenges Jesus.

The ensuing conversation about living water is reminiscent of the literal-minded Nicodemus who, like this woman, had little comprehension that Jesus was speaking of spiritual realities. Yet Jesus is always aware of the woman's dignity. To her, Jesus is even lower than Jacob (cf. Luke 9:52-56), for whom the well was named; she does not recognize who is speaking to her. But to Jesus, she is a woman of infinite worth, so much so that he completely dispenses with the social customs of the day.

Jesus then refocuses the conversation on the woman's personal life. He does not do this to shame or mock her, but in order to establish their respective true identities. By telling the woman who she is, Jesus enables her to see who he is. Jesus is not standing in judgment of her questionable marriage and domestic history. She is amazed by this man who knows so much about her. He is obviously more than a thirsty Jew who speaks cryptically about living water. But she still tries to turn the conversation away from herself by bringing up the subject of worship. Her ploy fails; Jesus knows exactly where she stands, between two mountains—Mount Gerizim, "the Mount of Blessing," and Mount Ebal, "the Mount of Cursing" (Deut. 11:26-30). He seems to know also that much of her life has been exclusively under the Mount of Cursing!

Jesus is even willing to let the topic of conversation change again, but he still includes her in his discourse: "Woman, believe me, the hour is coming when you will worship the Father neither on this mountain nor in Jerusalem . . . , when the true worshipers will worship the Father in spirit and truth" (vv. 21, 23). The issue is not to which husband she *belongs* (and in Jesus' time women were considered the property of their husbands) but whether she is open to the influence of the Mount of Blessing and is as such willing to become a true child of God the Father. Only those who worship in spirit and in truth can make this claim. Her past life and her relationship with the Samaritan law make no difference. The question is, Does she recognize the one with whom she is speaking? Does she know that she too is claimed by God as a child of God? The scene started out with Jesus asking her for physical water; it closes with the woman making a transformative move by seeking the spiritual water that Jesus offers.

By themselves, these verses make a wonderful story on which a preacher may base a sermon. But perhaps churchgoers would be short-changed if they were not given the opportunity to hear the rest of the story. For it is here that we see the woman witnessing to Christ; in the excitement of her newfound faith, she is given to some exaggeration ("Come and see a man who told me everything I have ever done!" [v. 29]). Yet neither the shock of the disciples nor the possibility of looking foolish to or incurring the wrath of the other Samaritans deters her. Jesus is not like the other Jews who degrade her and look upon her as impure; he has given her a new identity apart from her law. Because of her testimony, many come to believe in Jesus as the Messiah. But even more come to Christ on the merits of his own word (vv. 41-42). Not just one woman but a whole people are transformed by God; they are given a new identity by one who is himself not just a Jew but the Christ of Glory.

In the Old Testament lesson, we saw God act faithfully on behalf of God's people in spite of their unfaithfulness. In the Epistle, Paul explains the effects of God's love, that those who are justified by faith may "boast" in their right relationship with God. Now in the Gospel, this is illustrated for us by a woman who moves spontaneously (cf. Nicodemus) from curse to blessing and comes to faith. Thus she finds a new identity that is then shared with her entire town as well. As we move along in Lent, as we seek after God, we come to recognize who we are as well—children who are claimed by God, justified by faith, worshiping the Father in spirit and truth. For those who are stumbling along the path, preoccupied with sins of the past, this is good news indeed.

Fourth Sunday in Lent

Lutheran	Roman Catholic	Episcopal	Common Lectionary
Hos. 5:15—6:2	1 Sam. 16:1b, 6-7, 10-13a	1 Sam. 16:1-13	1 Sam. 16:1-13
Rom. 8:1-10	Eph. 5:8-14	Eph. 5:8-14	Eph. 5:8-14
Matt. 20:17-28	John 9:1-41	John 9:1-13, 28-38	John 9:1-41

This Sunday in Lent is the so-called *Laetare* Sunday because the Introit in the Latin liturgy begins unexpectedly with "rejoice." The day marks a celebration in the midst of sober Lenten observances. The worship asks the question, Are not all the judgments of God in human affairs ultimately occasions for rejoicing?

The drama of contrast and paradox in the life of faith, then, is the focus of the biblical texts of this Sunday. The ways of God confront and challenge human standards and expectations. The cause for celebration—for rejoicing—is this reversal of the usual, human view of this world.

In the Old Testament passage, 1 Sam. 16:1-13, the prophet Samuel is aroused by God from his grief over King Saul and directed to the sons of Jesse, from among whom God will select a successor. Samuel delights in each of the sons whom God passes over, "for the Lord does not see as mortals see; they look on the outward appearance, but the Lord looks on the heart" (v. 7b). When the pool of sons seems exhausted, Samuel asks if Jesse has other sons. The young David, who is watching the sheep, is beckoned, and God tells Samuel to anoint him as king.

In the New Testament Epistle, Eph. 5:8-14, the writer contrasts the life of darkness and the life in the light of Christ. The way of secrecy is death; the way of publicness brings the fruit of all that is good and right and true (vv. 9, 13-14). Against the judgments of this world, we are to walk as *children of light*, exposing an oppressive world of sinfulness (v. 11). (Those using the Lutheran lectionary should consult the Fifth Sunday in Lent, the New Testament Epistle.)

In the New Testament Gospel, John 9:1-41, those who appear disadvantaged are not to be judged as sinful—the usual judgment by persons in this world. In the light of Jesus, those who are "blind" can see, but those who profess to "see clearly" in this world become blind (vv. 39-41). Instead, we are directed to do the works of Jesus, the light of the world, and to worship him (vv. 35b-38).

FIRST LESSON: 1 SAMUEL 16:1-13

The First Lesson harks back to a time of transition in ancient Israel's political structure—the loose federation of tribes seemed no longer viable. This awareness caused the Israelites to clamor for a king (see 1 Sam. 10:19), but they quickly discovered that kings also provided serious problems. The principal source for 1 Samuel 16 is what form critics have simply called "the Late Source," which generally was *not* impressed with monarchial rule. The Late Source was itself edited by the Deuteronomic school, which emphasized not the centralization of political leadership in the monarchy, but the centrality of the Law and one place of worship. Nevertheless, the 1 Samuel 16 account of David's anointing makes plain the simple truth that the ways or standards of God usually contrast with those of human beings. This passage is filled with such contrasts, and the preacher may want to pay special attention to the paradoxical aspects of the story.

The anointing of David by Samuel follows the pattern established in 1 Sam. 10:17-27 (also Late Source) when Saul is the first king to be set apart. The selection process, however, is not by "popular acclaim" (human standards), but by divine discernment that escapes even the judge-priest Samuel (16:6-7). The penchant on the part of political rulers to disobey God's commands was evident in Saul's rule; such disobedience prompted the need for a new servant-king. Significantly (and the early church took note of this), Samuel anoints David in the city of Bethlehem.

The drama of the story is worth recapturing in summary form. It opens with God's commissioning Samuel, who laments over the divine rejection of Saul. Now, God tells Samuel to go to Bethlehem to select a new king from the sons of "Jesse the Bethlehemite" (vv. 1-2). Samuel is reluctant at first, in part because he fears that King Saul will get word of the trip and kill him. God insists that Samuel proceed at once to Bethlehem, but to do so under the pretext that his mission is merely one of priestly intercession. Even the elders of the city are troubled upon seeing that Samuel has arrived in town (vv. 4b-5); they come to meet him "trembling" and asking, "Do you come in peace?" Samuel assures them that his mission is a peaceful one, no matter what they might suspect or have heard about his estrangement with King Saul. Samuel invites the elders, along with Jesse and his sons, to participate in the communal sacrifice (*zabah*).

That scene one (vv. 1-5) closes on the note of sacrifice is reminiscent of the matter about which King Saul had been scolded, namely, "Surely, to obey is better than sacrifice" (1 Sam. 15:22). The way is now clear for Samuel's true mission to Bethlehem. He seeks to anoint one who truly and fully is obedient to God.

Scene two has its own suspense, created by the human (in contrast to divine) expectations or standards of Samuel. Immediately, Samuel is impressed beyond measure with Eliab, one of Jesse's sons; evidently Eliab was physically striking. Samuel must have said something to himself like "Surely, this is God's anointed!" (v. 6). This superficial presumption, however, provokes a stern rebuke from God: "Do not look on his appearance or on the height of his stature" (v. 7b). In other words: Do not be so superficial as you do your work on this solemn, divine commission! God then tells Samuel that "the Lord does not see as mortals see; they look on the outward appearance, but the Lord looks on the heart" (v. 7c-d; cf. Lev. 19:15; Matt. 22:16d; Gal. 2:6b; James 2:1-4).

How paradoxical: On the one hand, Samuel is a priest and prophet; on the other hand, he needs to be so instructed. Evidently, Samuel, like all of us, needs to be tutored anew in the extraordinary ways of God. The point is applicable in all times: The most important matters are often those that are not on the surface. That which can be seen or measured empirically on a human scale is not the uppermost; rather, the inner world of intent, integrity, and character—the very things that we cannot discern except by inference—is the most important.

The often-quoted "I Have a Dream" speech by Dr. Martin Luther King, Jr., makes this point precisely: "I have a dream that my four children will one day live in a nation where they will not be judged by the color of their skin, but by the content of their character" (Washington, D.C., August 1963). In ironic contrast, the black writer Shelby Steele entitled his book *The Content of Our Character* even though the "contents" of his book is a litany of bashing affirmative action and civil rights legislation—precisely those measures that gave substance to Dr. King's dream! How often do we love the dreams, but hate the means? This is Samuel—and us.

Samuel's scene in Bethlehem continues as the sons of Jesse are paraded before him, one by one. Each one is passed over by God, and Samuel concludes that someone is missing. The original selection process did not even include the one to be selected. The youngest, David, is then summoned from his task of "tending the sheep" (cf. John 21:15-17), while the company waits to be seated until he arrives. Given David's absence from the original proceedings, it is apparent that his father thought him insignificant. Yet by the Father's standards, he was about to become the anointed one of Israel. The description of David on that occasion is imprecise in the Hebrew, but is accurately rendered: "Now he was ruddy, and had beautiful eyes, and was handsome" (v. 12). While David's outward appearance is pleasant, he lacks impressive physical stature, maturity of years, and a commanding voice. This theme of obscure beginnings can be compared with Saul's anointing (1 Samuel 9–10), but we soon learn that David, unlike Saul, has inner as well as outer substance (1 Samuel 17–19). Thus, David is a prospective leader after God's own heart (13:14).

The scene closes when God commissions Samuel to anoint young David as king. Even though this anointing is public, more than a little time will pass before he is enthroned as king of both Judah (2 Sam. 2:11) and Israel (2 Sam. 5:3). At David's first anointing, the Spirit "rushed mightily upon him" and then "gripped" (*titzlakh*) him from that day onward (1 Sam. 16:13), indicating that "the Lord was with him" (16:18; 18:12, 14, 28). Then Samuel returns home to Ramah (16:13; cf. Jer. 31:15).

Placed in a worship context, the motif of the least likely prospect becoming the appointed one recounts the ways of God in Hannah's song: God "raises up the poor from the dust; he lifts the needy from the ash heap, to make them sit with princes and inherit a seat of honor. For the pillars of the earth are the Lord's, and on them he has set the world" (1 Sam. 2:8). Second Isaiah continues the theme of the anointing of David by contrasting human and divine judgments: "For my thoughts are not your thoughts, nor are your ways my ways, says the Lord. For as the heavens are higher than the earth, so are my ways higher than your ways" (Isa. 55:8-9a). Therefore, the seemingly least are not to be overlooked or ignored.

SECOND LESSON: EPHESIANS 5:8-14

(For Rom. 8:1-10, see the Fifth Sunday in Lent.)

Although Ephesians claims to be written by Paul (1:1; 3:1; 4:1), and some of his favorite themes—salvation by grace through faith not works (2:8-9) and "one body and one Spirit" (4:4), for example—appear, the language, style, and theological development of these themes suggest that the work was written by a disciple of Paul, perhaps around 85 C.E.

The text from Ephesians is part of a larger unit (4:1—6:20). This larger unit is filled with practical and ethical instructions (*paraenesis*), which are usually found at the end of Pauline letters (e.g., Col. 3:1—4:6; Galatians 5–6; Romans 12–14). This unit develops the practical implications of the Christian faith that has been expounded in the hymns, prayers, and baptismal instruction of the first part (chaps. 1–3).

The immediate context (4:17—5:20) reads like a homily on Christian living addressed to new converts. Analogies are drawn from baptism (4:22-25, 30), and the members of the audience seem to be struggling with their new identity (4:14-16; 5:1-5; cf. 2:1-7), much as recent converts might.

Whether delivered to catechumens or to candidates for baptism or to a mature Christian community, the passage contains a bold ethical challenge: to walk as *children of light* (cf. Gen. 1:3; John 1:5; 2 Cor. 4:6) in a world of darkness, to pursue goodness, justice, and truth in a world of oppression. For all Christians, this strategic injunction suggests we be "wise as serpents and innocent as doves" (Matt. 10:16).

Indeed, many Christians for centuries have pursued justice and truth with the shrewdness of snakes and the innocence of doves. Dr. Martin Luther King, Jr. wisely implemented these principles in the cause he championed for the freedom of all peoples:

> But there is something that I must say to my people who stand on the warm threshold which leads into the palace of justice. In the process of gaining our rightful place we must not be guilty of wrongful deeds. Let us not seek to satisfy our thirst for freedom by drinking from the cup of bitterness and hatred. We must forever conduct our struggle on the high plane of dignity and discipline. We must not allow our creative protest to degenerate into physical violence. Again and again we must rise to the majestic heights of meeting physical force with soul force. (Washington, D.C., August 1963).

Such "soul force" and such noble actions expose the ugly deeds of oppression like a bright, shining beacon.

This connects directly with the passage's opening: "For once you were darkness, but now in the Lord you are light. Live as children of light" (Eph. 5:8). And this contrast between the former state or condition and the new identity of the believer has already been set forth: "Remember that you were at that time without Christ, being aliens from the commonwealth of Israel, and strangers to the covenants of promise, having no hope and without God in the world. But now in Christ Jesus you who once were far off have been brought near by the blood of Christ" (2:12-13).

Placed in a worship context, the refrain (5:8a) on the sharp contrast between the former life apart from God and the new life in Christ is a wake-up call to new life, renewed illumination, and action: "Sleeper, awake! Rise from the dead, and Christ will shine on you" (Eph. 5:14; cf. Rom. 13:11-12). The problem is that the more comfortable our faith becomes, the more indifferent we are to our former condition and our present calling.

Instead, Christ is "the light of the world" (John 8:12; 9:5), and his followers are called "the light of the world" and are to let their lights shine forth in the world (Matt. 5:14-16). As the moon reflects the sun, so are Christians to reflect the light of Christ or to be bearers of his light.

GOSPEL: JOHN 9:1-41

The granting of sight to a man born blind occurs in the first major part of John's Gospel (chaps. 2–12). In this part are the "signs" (e.g., 2:11, 23; 4:54; 6:14; 7:31; 9:16; 11:47; 12:37) that Jesus is the Word made flesh, seen by means of his public ministry. The Gospel's final editor utilizes word play (e.g., 3:8; 11:11-13), paradox (8:37; 9:29), irony (8:22; 11:48-50), and motifs of misunderstanding (7:35-36; 11:11-12, 23-24) to achieve dramatic effect. Suspense is accomplished by allusions to the "hour" (2:4; 8:20) or "time" (7:6, 8, 30) of Jesus that is about to arrive and by the unbelief and hatred of the Jews and the world (5:16-18, 42-47; 8:37-59; 10:19-20, 31-33). The schemes and attempts to kill Jesus seem both to jeopardize (8:59; 10:31-33, 39; 11:8) and expedite (11:47-53) his accomplishing his mission. The remainder of John's Gospel, beginning with the farewell discourses (14:1—17:26), prepares the church for a glorious passion (18:1—19:42) and the threefold resurrection report (20:1-31).

The contrast in our passage between physical and spiritual blind-ness—like the Epistle's contrast between darkness and light—should be taken as an illustration of the profound drama of the human-divine paradox; it should not be used to demean those who are differently abled or not white or Jews. This drama unfolds in six suspenseful scenes. Throughout, we see the mounting tension between the truly "blind" Pharisees and those who come to believe in Jesus because they now "see" in a new way.

In the first scene (9:1-5), Jesus and his disciples see a young man who has been blind from birth. (We are not told how they know this, but the disciples' question in 9:2 confirms Jesus' own observation in 9:1). The resulting question ("Who sinned, this man or his parents?") assumes the ancient belief that suffering in this life is the result of divine punishment, justly rendered to the sufferer because of the person's own sins or those of parents or ancestors (Exod. 20:5; Lam. 5:7; Ezek. 18:2; Job 4:8; Pss. 51:5; 58:3; John 9:34). In good prophetic fashion (Jer. 31:29-30; Ezek. 18:2-5, 20), however, Jesus dismisses this so-called retribution. Instead, he views the malady as an occasion for God's work to be manifested in or through the blind man (cf. John 11:4). This pronouncement anticipates the sixth miraculous "sign" that Jesus performs. What seems to be a hopeless and fixed situation from a human standpoint is actually an opportunity for God's action. The scene continues with Jesus delivering a short maxim on seizing the opportunity of the moment "while it is still day" (cf. Jer. 13:16) and concludes (John 9:5) with Jesus' "I am" (*ego eimi*) utterance, reiterating what he had stated earlier: "I am the light of the world" (see 8:12).

In the second scene (9:6-7a), as in other healing stories, the therapy for the malady is provided, and proof of restoration to health is given (vv. 7b-12). Typical of the Johannine motif of misunderstanding (3:4), the neighbors are baffled. They question the man's identify (Is it really the blind beggar?) and inquire about the healing (How did it happen?) and further about the healer (Who is he?).

In the third scene (9:13-17), the human incredulity to God's work continues. Recalling the scenario from an earlier "sign" (5:9-12; cf. Mark 3:2), the Pharisees draw attention to the fact that the healing occurred on the Sabbath (9:16). Some judge Jesus as "not from God" because he broke God's Law. In a typical rabbinic manner, another raises the question of how Jesus can perform a sign from God when he has sinned against God's Law. A public controversy results (cf. 7:43).

The man is interrogated further about the healer's identity, and his sight leads to a new insight: "He [Jesus] is a prophet" (9:17b).

In the fourth scene (9:18-23), the Jewish authorities interrogate the parents of the man who was healed. Showing the symptoms of "spiritual myopia," the authorities do not believe the sign until the identity of the man is confirmed by the parents. When interrogated about how he was healed, the parents recommend that the authorities speak with the man themselves because he is of an accountable age, that is, over thirteen years old. The narrator comments that the parents feared expulsion from the synagogue for acknowledging Jesus as Messiah (cf. 12:42; 16:2). This comment seems to reflect a situation of tension between Jews and Jewish Christians more characteristic of the years after Jesus' life, perhaps 80-90 C.E. (cf. Rev. 2:9; 3:9).

In the fifth scene (John 9:24-27), a paradox emerges with comic aspects. The authorities interrogate the man a second time in order to elicit a confession from him (cf. Josh. 7:19) and to discredit Jesus as a sinner. But the man will not be wrenched from his experience of grace: "I do not know whether he [Jesus] is a sinner. One thing I do know, that though I was blind, now I see" (v. 25). He even refuses to be intimidated by further questioning: "I have told you already [how I was healed], and you would not listen. Why do you want to hear it again? Do you also want to become his disciples?" (v. 27). The paradox is that one who is unschooled sees whereas those in the know do not understand. The comic element is that the one examined becomes the examiner. His question and the reversal of the situation infuriate these "authorities," who now ridicule the man: "You are his disciple, but we are disciples of Moses. We know that God has spoken to Moses [Num. 12:6-8], but as for this man, we do not know where he comes from" (John 9:28-29). The replies of the healed man reveal the truth behind this apparent contradiction: Even though Jesus opened the man's eyes, these questioners do not know from whence he comes (cf. 5:45-47; 8:14).

The man to whom sight has been given stands before them as living proof of God's work in their midst. Yet, they cannot see it. Using the same type of argumentation that condemned Jesus as a sinner (9:16, 24), the man with great insight proceeds to show that Jesus, on the contrary, must be devout and from God in order to heal as he did (vv. 31-33; cf. Prov. 15:8, 29). But refusing to acknowledge the validity of the man's argument or the mercy shown in his healing, his accusers cast him out (9:34b, 35) of their considerations. These religious experts who claim to "see clearly" the ways of God thereby demonstrate their "blindness" (vv. 40-41).

In the sixth scene (9:35-41), the sight of the blind man and the blindness of the religious leaders are confirmed. Like one newly baptized (v. 7), and like a catechumen progressively instructed in the faith, the blind man first regards Jesus as a man (v. 11), next as a prophet (v. 17), then as one sent from God (v. 33), next as a heavenly Son of man (v. 35), and finally as the Lord worthy of worship (v. 38).

Jesus' paradoxical saying about coming into this world for judgment so "that those who do not see may see, and those who do see may become blind" (v. 39; cf. Isa. 6:9-10; Matt. 13:13-17) effectively summarizes the story. By refusing to acknowledge their blindness, the religious leaders confirm their imperception (John 9:40-41). The ways of God are hidden from the enlightened and revealed to the blind. For those who pursue that which is good, just, and true, this ironic truth may provide some helpful insight.

Placed in a worship context, this passage leads us again to Isa. 55:8-9, "For my thoughts are not your thoughts, nor are your ways my ways, says the Lord." The ways of God confront and challenge human standards and expectations. The cause for celebration—for rejoicing— is this reversal of the usual, human view of this world.

The preacher will need to analyze the current personal, social, and cultural forces that lead Christians into confusion or despair or oversight of God's workings. What is clear from all the texts of this Sunday, however, is that God is actively working to turn things upside down. Human reasons and judgments are being converted. Again, exactly how God is working to reshape our reasoning needs careful attention. But are not all the judgments of God in human affairs ultimately occasions for rejoicing?

Fifth Sunday in Lent

Lutheran	Roman Catholic	Episcopal	Common Lectionary
Ezek. 37:1-3, 11-14	Ezek. 37:12-14	Ezek. 37:1-3, 11-14	Ezek. 37:1-14
Rom. 8:11-19	Rom. 8:8-11	Rom. 6:16-23	Rom. 8:6-11
John 11:1-53	John 11:1-45	John 11:18-44	John 11:(1-16) 17-45

Many clergy—with Palm Sunday, Good Friday, and Easter in plain view—may be tempted to preach on an isolated individual's resurrection with these texts as illustrations. The biblical passages, however, point in a different direction: The lost hope and separation, even bondage, that many persons experience in the present need to be addressed with a word of hope and liberation, with both spiritual and social implications for us all.

In the Old Testament passage, Ezek. 37:1-14, the prophet is instructed to preach to the "whole house of Israel" (v. 11), both in exile and at home in Judah, that they shall be returned "from their graves" to the land of Israel. This passage already strains forward subtly to the Christian emphasis of a collective resurrection that inescapably lies ahead.

In the New Testament Epistle, Rom. 8:1-19, Paul contrasts the *present* bondage and sufferings with the coming glory to be revealed (vv. 18-19), noting that "all who are led by the Spirit of God are children of God . . . and if children, then heirs, heirs of God and joint heirs with Christ" (vv. 14, 17). (Or, in Rom. 6:16-23, Paul again emphasizes the *present* situation: "But now that you have been freed from sin and enslaved to God, the advantage you get is sanctification" [v. 22].)

Then, in the New Testament Gospel, John 11:1-44, the present time is cut short and filled with grief in the death of Lazarus: Many of the Jews had come to console Mary and Martha (v. 19); Mary and Martha each tell Jesus that their brother would not have died had Jesus been present (vv. 21, 32). In verse 35, we have the shortest verse within the New Testament: "Jesus wept" (here also is one of the two times that Jesus weeps [see Luke 19:41]). Then, in verse 37, even some in the crowd ask, "Could not he who opened the eyes of the blind have kept this man from dying?" After Jesus calls Lazarus back from the dead, he commands that Lazarus be unbound from his funeral wrappings (v. 44)—"those who walk during the day do not stumble, because they see the light of the world" (v. 9b).

FIRST LESSON: EZEKIEL 37:1-14

The prophet or editor arranged the book of Ezekiel in three large sections. The first (chaps. 1–24) contains Ezekiel's oracles of God's judgment on Israel. The second (chaps. 25–32) gathers up his prophecies of judgment against foreign nations. The third (chaps. 33–38) portrays a time of salvation, offering hope to a despairing people.

Second Kings 24:1-7 reviews the political events of 587–586 B.C.E. that led to the second exile and execution of the royal lineage (cf. Jer. 39:1-10; 52; 2 Chron. 36:11-21). Jerusalem was torched and sacked— and the Temple emptied of its precious treasures and burned (2 Kings 25:8-21). Then, the remaining population (except for "the poorest people of the land" [ʿam ha ʾarets] left to till the soil and tend the vineyards) were exiled to Babylon (Jer. 52:29 numbers only 832 persons).

The vision in Ezek. 37:1-14 contains an image (vv. 1-10) and an interpretation (vv. 11-14) addressed to these exiles. (For other visions, see Ezek. 1:1—3:15; 8:1—11:25; 40:1—48:35.) The prophet reports a dramatic vision in which God's hand has led the prophet out to a plain that is strewn with "very dry" bones. In this vision, God does not appear, but asks the rhetorical question, "Mortal, can these bones live?" or, literally, "Son of man, can these bones come to life again?" The prophet defers to God's knowledge and thereby presupposes the affirmative answer. Then God commands the prophet to prophesy— that is, speak the divinely given message—to these bones as if he truly believes it will make a difference! God's message then follows in the vision. At the conclusion of this message, which the prophet has repeated to the bones in this vision, a noisy rustling occurs in which each bone moves closer to its other ("bone to its bone"). This passage has traditionally captivated the black church, especially during the period of American slavery and its aftermath. The passage seems to have epitomized the hope of faith despite empirical evidence to the contrary (see the comments on "hope," in the Third Sunday in Lent, the Second Lesson).

The image given in this vision (vv. 1-10) is a bone-strewn field coming back to life. In the interpretation (vv. 11-14), the scene shifts to a graveyard ("I am going to . . . bring you up from your graves"; literally, "I will open your graves and bring you out of your graves"). The context also shifts as the prophet is now commanded to preach to God's people (vv. 11, 12). Nowhere is the prophet commanded to share with this people the spectacle of the dry bones. Not even the hinge-pin of this text (v. 11) is part of the proclamation.

Verse 11, however, provides the central clue to the text's procla-mation: "Mortal, these bones are the whole house of Israel. They say, 'Our bones are dried up, and our hope is lost; we are cut off completely' " (v. 11). All the hopeless events of the preceding years have been com-pressed into the single image of dry bones. Using bones as an image of the entire person, for praise or lament, takes up the language of the Psalms: "All my bones shall say, 'O Lord, who is like you? You deliver the weak from those too strong for them, the weak and needy from those who despoil them' " (Ps. 35:10); "Be gracious to me, O Lord, for I am in distress. . . . For my life is spent with sorrow, and my years with sighing; my strength fails because of my misery, and my bones waste away" (Ps. 31:9, 10). Perhaps Prov. 17:22 provides the closest parallel: A cheerful heart is a good medicine, but a downcast spirit dries up the bones."

One need not assume that the vision was prompted by actually coming across a battle scene; it is equally plausible that the need of the exiled people gave rise to the prophet's vision from God and the divine command to proclaim. Just as God can call together bleached bones in a valley, regenerate living flesh, and summon breath from the winds, so also can God open up graves in this foreign land and reas-semble a people in their homeland ("to the land of Israel" [v. 12]; "your own soil" [v. 14]).

The text's interpretative portion is the reconstruction or reassemblage or resuscitation or revivification of a people, as the refrain, "O my people," repeated twice (v. 12, 13), illustrates. A dead, "vast multitude" (v. 10) has now become God's people. To this is added probable allusions to the Exodus: "I am going to bring you up . . . and bring you back to the land of Israel" (v. 12; the same verb is used, for example, in 1 Sam. 12:6 and Hos. 12:14). Thus, a double recognition formula is used in conjunction with a twofold promise of life and land in verse 14: " 'I will put my spirit within you, and you shall live, and I will place you on your own soil; then you shall know that *I, the Lord, have spoken and will act,'* says the Lord" (emphasis added).

Placed in a worship context, this unusual visionary event seems intended to stir up despairing people in all racial-ethnic groups to be God's people and to hope in God's promises. Perhaps the closest situation today to that of the Hebrews in Babylon is the plight of black people in South Africa or of Native American, Latinos, and blacks in the United States. The oppression of entire groups of persons, relegating them to inferior or lower social classes, and the plight of women, especially in the two-thirds world, might also be given attention. Blatant and subtle forms of racism and sexism are still experienced, as "affirmative action" is converted into the scare language of "racial preference" and as a declining economy seeks "scapegoats."

In any case, the harshness applied to a once-prosperous people (Ezek. 15, 16, 20, 23) is now absent; life is here proclaimed without preconditions. The prophet's commission then—no less than the pastor's today—is to proclaim: "Thus says the Lord" (v. 12).

SECOND LESSON: ROMANS 8:1-19

In the discussion of the First Sunday in Lent, Rom. 5:12—8:39 was identified as Part Two of Paul's epistle. The entire epistle is a working out of Rom. 1:16: "For . . . the gospel . . . is the power of God for salvation to everyone who has faith, to the Jew first and also to the Greek." In Part One, "The Righteousness of God," Paul unfolds how a person through faith is righteous. In Part Two, he explicates in these "freedom chapters" how a person, righteous through faith, shall live. Here, the "power of God for salvation" means first that the believer is *freed from* God's wrath because the reign of grace is as wide as the reign of sin, and far more powerful (5:12-21). Second, the believer is *freed from* sin (6:1-23). Third, the believer is *freed from* the Law (7:1-25). Fourth, the believer is freed from death because he or she is *freed for* a new life in the Spirit who brings freedom, power, present help, and future glory (8:1-30).

For this Sunday, the Episcopal lectionary centers on Rom. 6:22— "But now that you have been *freed from* sin and enslaved to God, the advantage you get is sanctification. The end is eternal life" (emphasis added). The new life under grace is illustrated by slavery: The Christian is bound to a new Master. Because slavery is hardly the happiest of analogies, perhaps such a concept as "dependence" may make Paul's meaning usable in the present context. Yet we would misunderstand Paul if we assumed that the same old person now simply had a new owner or a different "crutch." Paul's point is that something fundamental has been changed in the believer: The old person ignored righteousness and worked (or played) hard to gain its due—"death" (vv. 20-21, 23). By contrast, the believer has "become obedient from the heart" (v. 17) and "has been set free from sin" (v. 18), receiving "the free gift of God" that is "eternal life in Christ Jesus our Lord" (v. 23).

In what follows this text, Paul compares the deliverance from sin and the Law to being subject to a marriage partner; the Christian's former marriage to the Law is ended because the sinful self has died in Christ and the new self, raised from the dead, is now wedded to Christ (7:1-6). This is summed up in Rom. 8:1-2: "There is therefore now no condemnation for those who are in Christ Jesus. For the law of the Spirit of life in Christ Jesus has set you free from the law of sin and death."

Romans 8:1-19 could be summarized as follows: The Law of the Spirit (v. 2) condemns sin in the flesh (v. 3); but believers are in the Spirit of Christ that determines what is carnal or spiritual (v. 9) and whose indwelling marks the death of the body with respect to sin (v. 10). This Spirit guarantees life to mortal bodies, making us debtors (v. 11) and inheritors of adoption as "children" (v. 15) and able to withstand present sufferings because of the future glory that will be revealed (v. 19).

For lectionary traditions other than Episcopalians, only Rom. 8:11 is in common: "If the Spirit of him who raised Jesus from the dead dwells in you, he who raised Christ from the dead will give life to your mortal bodies also through his Spirit that dwells in you." Again we are reminded of Paul's thought of Adam and Christ (Rom. 5:12-21). Theodore Roosevelt's American notion of rugged individualism—that we are distinct persons accountable only to ourselves despite living in the context of others—is completely alien to Paul's thought. One need not seek a psychological explanation that connects us as individuals either to Adam or to Christ, nor an explanation that appeals to some "collectivity"—a total or amorphous aggregate of all individuals. These are not especially helpful. Rather Paul sets forth the idea of the body of sin and death to which we belong by nature ("in Adam") and the body of Christ into which we are incorporated by faith and baptism. Death, for Paul, does not merely cut the individual off from life; it is a universal power that rules over humanity, a powerful master—including wrath, sin, and the Law—that rules over human existence. The Spirit of Christ is the power that makes us alive, and here in Romans 8, the vindicating forces are also an inclusive reality: receiving God's love in Christ, being freed from sin through incorporation into Christ's body by baptism (Romans 6), being dead to the Law, and now being freed from death.

Only for one lectionary (Lutheran) does the Epistle reading move beyond Rom. 8:11. Nevertheless, a communal dimension is stressed in vv. 12-14 and should be kept in mind by all: "So then, brothers and sisters, we are debtors, not to the flesh . . . ; but if by the Spirit you put to death the deeds of the body, you will live. For all who are led by the Spirit of God are children of God."

Placed in a worship context, this passage should not be used merely to address the modern, personal, or individualistic fear of death. Here again, we might consider today's diverse marginalized and oppressed within our midst and within all of humanity who labor under "the sufferings of this present time," including wrath, sin, Law, and death (v. 18). Persons who work against structures of injustice are especially vulnerable, paradoxically, to being themselves treated with disdain, even rejection and abuse. Indeed, the paradox is heightened because many of the poor and oppressed are themselves caught in a web of sin and death. Paul's message disrupts the status quo. He speaks to Christians forthrightly: "To set the mind on flesh is death, but to set the mind on the Spirit is life and peace" (v. 6); "you are in the Spirit since the Spirit of God dwells in you" (v. 9); and God "who raised Christ from the dead will give life to your mortal bodies also through his Spirit that dwells in you" (v. 11).

GOSPEL: JOHN 11:1-44 (45-53)

The raising of Lazarus is the last and perhaps greatest miracle story or sign in John's Gospel. This sign brings the coming age into the present, "when the dead will hear the voice of the Son of God, and those who hear will live" (5:25, 26-29). It also sets the stage for Jesus' own death—"So from that day on they took counsel how to put him to death" (11:53)—and his resurrection.

The Synoptics do not contain this story, even though Lazarus, Martha, and Mary appear in Luke 10:38-42 (in a different context). Nor is the later story of the anointing at Bethany, where Mary washed Jesus' feet

(John 12:1-11), found in the Synoptics. The Synoptics, however, do offer resurrection stories: that of the daughter of Jairus (Mark 5:22-43) and that of the young man from Nain (Luke 7:11-17).

Several details in the narrative may seem odd to the reader. John's hearers apparently had knowledge of Mary's anointing Jesus' feet with perfume (John 12:1-3), and so this information is disclosed prior to the event (11:2). The message bearer suddenly is forgotten after the message is delivered (v. 3): "So the sisters sent a message to Jesus." The text is filled with "so" (*oun*) and "now," as is typical of John's narrative events (*oun* occurs fourteen times in the Greek version of this text). The emphasis is on decisiveness and immediacy, for time itself now seems to be passing quickly. Later, Martha tells Mary that "the teacher is . . . calling for you," even though Jesus says nothing like this in the text (v. 28).

One detail is quite surprising and the narrator is at pains to account for it: Jesus pauses after receiving the message. "Lord, he whom you love is ill" (v. 3) is countered by Jesus' own assessment: "This illness does not lead to death; rather it is for God's glory, so that the Son of God may be glorified through it" (v. 4). Even though Jesus loves Martha, Mary, and Lazarus, he waits two days longer (vv. 5-6). Yet, Jesus is fully aware that Lazarus has died (v. 14) and tells his disciples that for their sake—for their faith—Jesus was glad not to have been in Bethany at Lazarus' death (v. 15). Even this unfortunate occasion of a dear friend's death is an opportunity for Jesus to demonstrate in grand style the glory of God.

Verses 7-11a seem to be an insertion into a more primitive source. The announcement that Jesus intends to go to Judea, presumably for "God's glory" (v. 4), is countered by the disciples: "Rabbi, the Jews were just now trying to stone you, and are you going there again?" (v. 8; cf. 8:59; 10:39). Jesus answers a question with a question. The day with its twelve hours ignores the separate reality of night (and variation of the day's length according to seasons). The core of his response, according to Bultmann, is: "Whoever walks by day does not stumble; but if anyone walks by night, he stumbles." (The point at which Judas betrays Jesus makes reference to the night [13:30].) The response reported in the text is puzzling in its second part. To paraphrase: Those who walk during the day do not trip on loose stones because sunlight illuminates the uneven path, but those who walk at night often stumble because the human body provides no headlamp. In short, one will tend to grope and stumble in the darkness.

The Gospel writer connects day with life and night with death by means of this insertion (v. 7a, "after this," is repeated in v. 11a). Lazarus has "fallen asleep" and needs to be "awakened" (v. 11). Thus, a riddle is presented to the disciples in order to underscore their lack of knowledge in the face of Jesus' wisdom. "For your sake I am glad I was not there, so that you may believe. But let us go to him" (v. 15). "Sleep" is the euphemism for "has died" (vv. 13, 16). Jesus is glad because otherwise Lazarus would not have died but would have been healed (see 11:21-32) and an *opportunity for faith* lost. Even though the narrator of the original source might be convinced that a witness to a resurrection will come to faith more readily than one who observes a healing, the evangelist understands the Father's world to be entirely other than the mundane (cf. 20:24-28, where Thomas later doubts, and v. 29, in which Jesus affirms the blessedness of those who believe without seeing). Miracles, whether healings or a resurrection, point us to what Rudolph Otto has called "the idea of the Holy" and what Howard Thurman has termed the "disciplines of the Spirit." Here the resurrection of the spiritually dead to fellowship with God, to authentic life, is about to be displayed.

Upon their arrival in Bethany (v. 17), the disciples drop away from the narrative. It has been four days since Lazarus' death, and that is significant because of an ancient Jewish belief that the soul lingered near the body for three days after death. A period of four days makes mere resuscitation impossible.

Mourners from Jerusalem (vv. 18-19) arrive soon because of the short distance between Jerusalem and Bethany. They follow an ancient practice (2 Sam. 10:2) that was promoted in the day by rabbis. The protocol was intricate, beginning on the way home from the body's interment and lasting for seven days, with mourners constantly arriving at the house and the bereaved usually staying there. These Jewish mourners would later spread reports of the miracle in Jerusalem (John 11:45).

Martha, then Mary, go out to greet Jesus at the edge of town (v. 30). Again, how Martha received the news of Jesus' approach is unimportant (she "heard that Jesus was coming" [v. 20]). Martha expresses both her grief and her trust in Jesus: Had he been present, her brother would not have died because death must yield in his presence (v. 21) and because God even now grants Jesus' every petition (indirect request; v. 22). Jesus' response (v. 23) is open to two interpretations: Lazarus will be raised up in the end-time resurrection, or he will be raised up presently. The evangelist's own concerns are lurking behind the ensuing interchange, as Ernst Haenchen points out. The true resurrection occurs anytime that eyes are opened and faith is realized in the here and now—but not quite as Martha is expecting—as a body resuscitated. Martha seems to be asking that Jesus make an exception to the rule because she believes that Jesus has this power, except that for Jesus the present exception is the rule. Thus, in the text, John notes that Martha falls back on the traditional belief ("I know" [v. 24]; cf. Ezek. 37:1-20; John 5:25-29). But for the fourth evangelist, spiritual resurrection occurs in the moment of faith; bodily resurrection is an imitation of spiritual resurrection and becomes visible only in incidental times such as this one (Haenchen).

Jesus, however, ruptures this old, limited horizon: "I am the resurrection and the life" (v. 25a). Two affirmations follow: On the one hand, those who believe in Jesus in the present can receive no higher communion with God (v. 25b); and on the other hand, this communion is not interrupted by physical death (v. 26). Both are united in John 5:24: "Very truly, I tell you, anyone who hears my word and believes him who sent me has eternal life, and does not come under judgment, but has passed from death to life." Martha's liturgically stylized confession ends the scene (v. 27).

With that Martha exits and Mary enters the scene (vv. 28-31). Although nothing can be added in the ensuing dialogue (v. 32), the Gospel writer knows of the two sisters and needs to give space to both. Contrasting Martha's complaints with Mary's adoration makes too much of their different approaches. Instead, Mary's weeping allows the expression of Jesus' own grief (vv. 33, 35). Further, the mourners follow Mary and are therefore present to witness the following scene and raise again the fact that Jesus' presence would not have allowed Lazarus' death (v. 37).

That Jesus asks where Lazarus has been interred (v. 34) contrasts with the usual impression that Jesus is fully aware of things (for example, that Lazarus had died, earlier). At the command to remove the stone from the grave (v. 39), Martha has the thankless task of expressing doubt in the power of God and difficulty in conceiving so great a miracle (v. 40). Mention of the body's stench serves to heighten the scene—a decaying corpse raised to life. Jesus' words (vv. 41-42; for other prayers in John, see 12:27; 17:1-26) indicate that he knew in advance of the Father's fulfilling the request (cf. v. 41). Moreover, Jesus articulates thanks to the Father only so that those present will know that Jesus is sent by the Father (v. 42).

The miracle is brief: Jesus, the divine man, calls with a loud voice, "Lazarus, come out!" (v. 43), and Lazarus comes forth without stumbling, even though his face is wrapped with a cloth (v. 44). Why? "Those who walk during the day do not stumble, because they see the light of this world" (v. 9). Lazarus is to be unbound from his grave cloths (v. 44). Why? "Those who believe in me, even though they die, will live, and everyone who lives and believes in me will never die" (v. 25b-26). Whereas in previous signs, the meaning is given *after* the sign, here the meaning is given *prior to* the sign. Whereas in chapter 9, Jesus plays on the physical and spiritual meanings of eyesight (still present in this text), here resurrection from death to physical life is used to illustrate the gift of life in Jesus. In John 11:45-53, this sign places Jesus directly into confrontation with the authorities.

Placed in a worship context, this Gospel reading is meant as a present declaration or proclamation to all hearers: In Christ, God is at work liberating humans from all those forces that imprison and oppress all persons, not the least of which is death itself. Thus, a marvelous convergence seems present in the three readings for this Sunday. From the Old Testament lesson, the unusual visionary event seems intended to stir up despairing *groups* of people to be God's people and to hope in God's promises. From the New Testament Epistle, the preacher is also called to address groups—indeed, all humanity—that labor under "the sufferings of this present time," including wrath, sin, Law, and death.

In all three, but especially in the Epistle and the Gospels, it is worth repeating that persons who work against structures of injustice too often engage in a thankless task, being treated with disdain, even rejection and abuse. Nevertheless, even in the twilight of Lent, all of us are challenged to understand their work and to realign our spiritual disciplines with the continuing biblical mandate for justice and righteousness (Matt. 6:33; 2 Cor. 5:21). The church too often lacks courage and moral vision on the pressing issues of public policy. We are prepared for Holy Week with a strengthened "inner vision" that opens us for a new encounter with the passion and resurrection of Jesus, who became for us all—the Christ! This universal Christ invites one and all to become indeed "the righteousness" (justice) of God. The season of Lent prepares us for nothing less!